97ᴿ

*Basic
statistics*
for librarians

Basic
statistics
for librarians

2nd edition

I S SIMPSON
MA MInstP FIInfSc

Principal Lecturer
School of Librarianship and Information Studies
Newcastle upon Tyne Polytechnic

CLIVE BINGLEY LONDON

First published 1975
This revised edition published 1983

British Library Cataloguing in Publication Data

Simpson, Ian S.
    Basic statistics for librarians.—2nd ed.
    1. Mathematical statistics
    I. Title
    519.5'024092   QA276

    ISBN 0-85157-352-5

Typeset by Allset in 10 on 12 point Press Roman

1234568685848382

CONTENTS

Preface		7
Acknowledgements		9
Introduction		11
Part I Quantitative data		15
1	Presentation of quantitative data	17
2	Averages	30
3	Dispersion	40
4	Sampling	52
5	Statistics and parameters	62
6	Probability	68
7	Statistical testing	85
Part II Qualitative data		105
8	Presentation of qualitative data	107
9	Chi-squared test	119
Part III Qualitative/quantitative data		129
10	Presentation of qualitative/quantitative data	131
11	Indexes	140
12	Time series	149
13	Analysis of variance	159
Part IV Quantitative/Quantitative data		165
14	Presentation of quantitative/quantitative data	167
15	Correlation	174
16	Regression	187
Part V Mechanization		195
17	Computer packages	197
Further reading		213
Answers to examples		215

Appendices

1 Mathematical methods   219
2 Symbols used   224
3 Formulae used   226
4 Random numbers   229
5 t distribution   230
6 F distribution   231
7 χ^2 distribution   233
8 e^{-x} 234

Index   235

PREFACE

A sequence of thoughts not infrequently expressed by students of librarianship is: 'Statistics is concerned with numbers; numbers are to do with Mathematics; I never could cope with Mathematics; I cannot do Statistics'. It is true that a study of statistics involves some mathematics — but, at an elementary level of study of the subject, little more than the fundamental rules of arithmetic is required. Lack of success in 'O' level mathematics should not be taken, therefore, as an indication that statistics is going to be beyond understanding. In fact, a number of years of teaching statistics to students of librarianship on undergraduate, post-graduate, and post-experience courses has proved that the basic essentials of the subject are within the grasp of the majority, whatever their previous studies and aptitudes may have been. Statistics is more a matter of logical thinking and, as such, is as comprehensible to students of the arts as it is to the mathematician or scientist — in the same way as many good computer programmers have arts backgrounds and are not applied mathematicians as so often is assumed.

Of course, statistics can be studied to honours degree level and beyond and, at those levels, it is a highly complex subject. However, very few librarians have — or are expected to have — such a high level of expertise. If they have need to make use of more advanced statistical techniques, then they will consult a qualified statistician — just as they will consult an architect over the design of a new library, or a lawyer over legal matters arising in library operations, or a computer specialist over the mechanization of library housekeeping. But, in communicating with the specialist, it is important that the librarian should have some knowledge of the subject under discussion and, therefore, the purpose of this book is to give to librarians who are new to the subject an appreciation of statistics, its methods and applications. Fully fledged statisticians will not be created by assimilating its contents.

The book is intended as a text for students of librarianship, to provide them with sufficient familiarity with statistical methods to enable them to understand their utilization when referred to in specialized areas of study such as management of libraries and bibliometrics. Students may not acquire a full understanding of the underlying theory, but the rule-of-thumb methods of performing typical calculations which are given will provide patterns to be followed and applied to other similar problems. Collections of examples are included, some involving actual data and situations, others involving hypothetical data and situations which are simply illustrations of the use of the various procedures rather than real problems. Mastery of the procedures will help students to show that information collected in projects can be manipulated in order to lead to useful conclusions and will assist them to present information and results more effectively.

Practising librarians, who have hitherto relied on experience and intuition in their work but who are finding that today's increasing pressures and constraints demand more objective approaches, may also find that the text will give them a basic introduction to statistics on which they can subsequently build by reference to more advanced works.

In writing this text, I have taken the opportunity to incorporate topics which I have included in courses since the first edition of this work was published in 1975. These developments have followed useful discussions with a number of colleagues at the Newcastle upon Tyne School of Librarianship and Information Studies, in particular with Roger Woodhouse and Michael Heine who share the teaching of the Research Methods and Statistics courses. Experience gained through the good offices and facilities of Newcastle upon Tyne Polytechnic Computer Unit has enabled me to include the section on mechanization. I also welcomed comments from students who have completed courses under my guidance and I have naturally heeded their criticisms and difficulties so that future generations may benefit from their trials and tribulations. Last but not least, I must express my appreciation of the encouragement given to me by my wife, Mary, without which this book would not have been written.

I S Simpson
Newcastle upon Tyne
March 1982

8

ACKNOWLEDGEMENTS

The table of random numbers in Appendix 4 is reproduced with the permission of the Department of Statistics and Computer Science, University College, London, from Kendall and Babington-Smith's collection in the series 'Tracts for computers 24'. The t distribution in Appendix 5 and the χ^2 distribution in Appendix 7 are reproduced from Castle, W M *Statistics in small doses*, 1972, with the permission of the publishers Churchill Livingstone, Edinburgh, and the F distribution in Appendix 6 is reproduced by permission of the publishers, Charles Griffin & Co Ltd of London and High Wycombe, from David, F N *A first course in statistics*, 2nd ed, 1971.

I am also pleased to acknowledge the help given by the Borough Librarian of Gateshead and the City Librarian of Newcastle upon Tyne in providing statistics on library use that I have incorporated in various places in the text and in many of the examples. In other examples, use has been made of data that have been gleaned over the years from a variety of publications. References to the sources of these data were not recorded but I gladly acknowledge to the authors, whoever they may be, their value in providing more realistic problems to illustrate the subject matter of this text.

INTRODUCTION

To put a study of statistics into perspective, we should start by being as clear as possible about what is meant by the term. There are several definitions but a useful one given by the Shorter Oxford English Dictionary is that statistics are 'numerical facts or data collected and classified'. That leads us to find that data are things 'known or assumed as fact, and made the basis of reasoning or calculation'. Data have been collected in libraries for time immemorial and are commonly presented in annual reports, eg numbers of staff, numbers of readers, numbers of items stocked, numbers of items loaned etc, often with comparable figures for previous years. Whether such data are normally presented to best advantage and in the most helpful way is debatable. Graphs may be much more meaningful than lists of figures for conveying information to readers although, of course, they involve the expense of preparation and block-making for publication. Nevertheless, diagrams are an important means of communicating numerical facts and librarians should be familiar with both their preparation and their interpretation. However, such 'Descriptive Statistics' are perhaps the easy part of the subject. The more difficult part — the reasoning or calculation based on the data — is fundamental to decision-making. The economic pressures and constraints of the 1970s and 1980s have brought an increasing awareness that management of library and information services must be based on more objective evaluations of the factors involved rather than simply on the subjective experience and common sense of the manager concerned. He may feel that there are more readers using the library on certain days of the week than on others. He may feel that there were more readers using the library in a given period of time than in the corresponding period in the previous year. He may collect data on numbers of books issued each day or numbers of readers entering the library each week. Such data collection is easy, albeit tedious. But his feelings and mere record of numbers of issues or numbers of readers will not tell him whether the variations from hour to hour, day to day, week to week or year to year are sufficiently significant for him to vary the deployment or increase the number of staff, adjust the size of his book stock, alter the number of books per reader's ticket, close the library at certain times, and so on. Obviously, much more value will be derived from data if they can be interpreted and used for making management decisions than if they are simply presented for consumption in their raw state.

It seems appropriate to mention here the old adage according to Disraeli of there being 'lies, damned lies, and statistics'. Of course, the unscrupulous can fool the unwary with the way statistics are presented, manipulated or interpreted, but the blame should not be put on the statistics. It is all the more reason why librarians should be familiar with methods of data collection, data presentation and data interpretation.

Methods of data collection are more appropriate to a study of Research Methods, for which the reader should see, for example, texts by Line, Federer, and Bush and Harter. However, the reader should be aware that statistics presented are no better than the quality of the data collected. It is no use coming to decisions regarding library use on the basis of a survey carried out only on a rainy day nor a survey carried out immediately prior to examinations or during vacations.

But even if data are collected well, statistics can readily acquire a bad name if the data are badly interpreted or if conclusions are drawn from partial information. It would be only too easy to castigate a librarian for profligate spending on stock as shown by data on expenditure in successive years. Yet a comparison of those data with the book cost index might show that he should be congratulated for keeping below the rate of inflation. The statistical techniques are satisfactory; it is their application which may be suspect.

Having drawn attention to such problems of interpretation and abuse of statistics, no further treatment of those aspects of the subject will be given in this text. Nevertheless, it is hoped that, as the reader becomes familiar with the statistical methods described, the pitfalls and their avoidance will be borne in mind. For readable expositions on the mis-use of statistics, reference may be made to the books by Campbell, Huff, and Kimble.

Since statistics are concerned with data, readers should appreciate at the outset that data consist of observations of some attribute which varies from one observation to another. Thus, shelves in a library have

12

the attribute of storing books and, as we go from one shelf to another, we note that the number of books on a shelf varies. One shelf might have 20 books, another shelf might have 24 books, another shelf might have 25 books, and so on. The number of books per shelf is a *variable*. However, there are two types of variable, a quantitative variable and a qualitative variable.

A quantitative variable involves a counting operation at each observation. For example, the number of books per shelf is a quantitative variable because, for each shelf that is observed, the number of books on it is counted.

Similarly, the daily issues from a library is a quantitative variable because, for each day that is observed, the number of books issued is counted.

Also, the time taken to carry out a search for information is a quantitative variable because, for each search that is carried out, the number of minutes spent on the task may be counted.

In contrast, a qualitative variable involves the allocation of an observation to a particular group or category according to the attribute of interest. For example, the subject of a book is a qualitative variable because each book that is observed can be allocated to a category according to whether it is a history book, a chemistry book, a geography book, and so on.

Similarly, the type of document is a qualitative variable because, as each one is accessioned, it can be noted as a textbook, a report, a patent specification, or a periodical.

Also, the language of a publication is a qualitative variable because, as each document is inspected, it may be found to be in French, or German, or Russian, or Chinese.

It is important that the type of variable should be recognized easily and clearly since the form of presentation of data and the statistical treatment of data depend on the type of variable involved. Some observations involve quantitative data only and some involve qualitative data only but, in some circumstances, observations may include both qualitative and quantitative data whilst, in others, two quantitative variables may be noted at each observation. Each of these situations is dealt with in the text, with explanations of the appropriate methods of presenting the data in tabular and/or graphical form and of the relevant statistical operations. Sufficient theory is included to give some understanding of the methods described and as few assumptions as possible are made regarding basic knowledge required. Readers who feel that

13

they need revision of the necessary basic arithmetic and methods of performing calculations might usefully refer to Appendix 1.

Examples
Are the following variables quantitative or qualitative?
1   The height of a book
2   The age of a report
3   The sex of a library user
4   The age of a library user
5   The cost of a paperback
6   The distance from a reader's home to the library
7   The frequency of use of a document
8   The place of residence of a library user
9   The need for re-binding a book
10   The size of population served by a library

Part I

QUANTITATIVE DATA

Chapter 1

PRESENTATION OF QUANTITATIVE DATA

There is a number of possible ways of presenting quantitative data, depending on the quantity and nature of the data and the type of information that it is required to convey.

Linear array
If the number of observations of a variable is small, they could be recorded as the raw data. For example, the number of books issued on ten different days in a library were:

329 247 262 356 278 280 240 284 304 220

However, the values of the variable can be more easily assimilated if the data are presented in an *array* in ascending or descending order of magnitude:

220 240 247 262 278 280 284 304 329 356

Graphically, they would simply be represented by a linear array of dots as shown in Figure 1.1 since there is only one observation of each value of the variable.

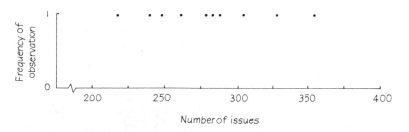

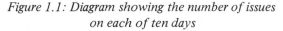

Figure 1.1: Diagram showing the number of issues on each of ten days

17

If there should be a second observation of a particular value of the variable, the dot would appear at twice the height.

So, few observations are of little value from a statistical point of view, the only use being to give some indication of the spread of the variable. The difference between the highest and lowest values of the variable is known as the *range*. For the data in Figure 1.1, the range is 136, ie 356-220.

Frequency table

As the number of observations increases, a record of the raw data becomes less and less manageable. Thus, observation of the number of books on eighty shelves in a library provided the data in Figure 1.2 in the order in which the data were collected.

25	23	23	24	23	29	22	27	25	21
27	24	24	28	23	23	28	24	25	23
28	24	25	27	23	19	25	22	24	20
28	25	27	23	22	21	27	28	26	21
26	27	26	25	30	25	23	23	20	25
29	21	21	26	20	23	26	21	24	30
29	21	22	23	22	26	25	23	26	26
23	26	28	24	19	24	24	24	25	25

Figure 1.2: Number of books per shelf – raw data

Even putting the data into an array is not much help, as can be seen in Figure 1.3.

19	19	20	20	20	21	21	21	21	21
21	21	22	22	22	22	22	23	23	23
23	23	23	23	23	23	23	23	23	23
23	24	24	24	24	24	24	24	24	24
24	24	25	25	25	25	25	25	25	25
25	25	25	25	26	26	26	26	26	26
26	26	26	27	27	27	27	27	27	28
28	28	28	28	28	29	29	29	30	30

Figure 1.3: Number of books per shelf – array

However, the data can be presented more concisely and in a form that enables the reader to detect some sort of pattern. Figure 1.4 shows the data from Figure 1.3 set out in two lines. On the top line are all the values of the variable (the number of books per shelf) in an array and on the bottom line is the number of times that each value of the variable was observed. The latter is referred to as the *frequency* and this form of presentation is known as a *frequency table*.

Number of books per shelf	19	20	21	22	23	24	25	26	27	28	29	30
Frequency of observation	2	3	7	5	14	11	12	9	6	6	3	2

Figure 1.4: Number of books per shelf – frequency table

It will be noted that the variable is the line in which the figures continue to increase in the array whilst the frequency is the line in which the figures rise or fall erratically. Thus, two shelves were observed, each with 19 books; three shelves were observed, each with 20 books, and so on. The total number of shelves observed is found by adding together all the frequencies, ie:

$$2 + 3 + 7 + 5 + 14 + 11 + 12 + 9 + 6 + 6 + 3 + 2 = 80$$

Relative frequency
A limitation of the frequency table is that the exact proportion of all the shelves that contain a given number of books cannot readily be seen. Thus, we can see that there are 14 shelves on each of which there are 23 books but is that a large or small proportion of the total number of shelves? That question can be answered by presenting the data in the form of a *relative frequency table*. Instead of showing the actual frequencies (as in Figure 1.4), relative frequencies are shown, calculated from the actual frequencies by the expression:

$$\text{Relative frequency} = \frac{\text{Actual frequency}}{\text{Sum of all the frequencies}}$$

Thus, the relative frequency of observing 23 books per shelf is $\frac{14}{80}$ or 0.175. The complete data are then as shown in Figure 1.5. We can now see immediately that there are 23 books per shelf on 0.175 (or nearly one-fifth) of all the shelves observed. Note also that the sum of all the relative frequencies is always unity.

19

Number of books per shelf	Relative frequency
19	0.0250
20	0.0375
21	0.0875
22	0.0625
23	0.1750
24	0.1375
25	0.1500
26	0.1125
27	0.0750
28	0.0750
29	0.0375
30	0.0250

Figure 1.5: Number of books per shelf
– relative frequency

Histograms

The data from a frequency table or from a relative frequency table can be presented graphically in the form of a *histogram*. The variable is always plotted on the horizontal axis and the frequency is always plotted on the vertical axis of the graph. Equal steps are marked off on the horizontal axis to represent the values of the variable and the number of observations of each value of the variable is represented by the height of a vertical column with its base on the horizontal axis. The data from Figure 1.4 are shown in the histogram of Figure 1.6.

Scrutiny of a histogram could help in decision-making. Suppose that a library hitherto had put no limitation on the number of books that a reader was allowed to borrow. A survey of borrowings may provide data such as shown in Figure 1.7.

If a ticket system were introduced and each reader were issued with only two tickets, a large number of readers would have to change their borrowing habits, whilst, if ten tickets were issued to each reader, it would not appear to be worth introducing a ticket system. From Figure 1.7, it will be clear that four tickets per reader would be an appropriate choice.

20

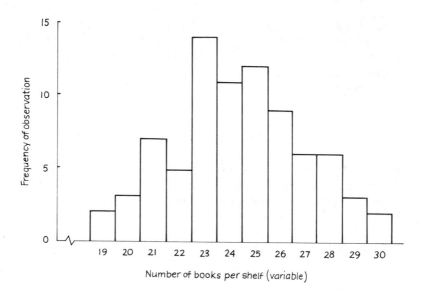

Figure 1.6: Number of books per shelf – histogram

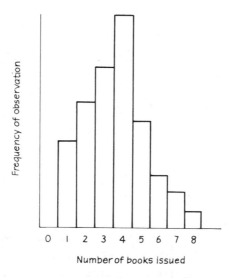

Figure 1.7: Histogram of number of books issued to readers

Frequency polygons
If two or more sets of data are to be compared — as, for example, the number of books per shelf in a fiction library as compared with the number of books per shelf in a non-fiction library — histograms could not satisfactorily be used since their superimposition would be confusing. Instead, a *frequency polygon* can be constructed by joining the points which, for a histogram, would be the mid-points of the tops of the columns (Figure 1.8). Note that the frequency polygon is continued at each end until it meets the horizontal axis. It will be apparent that two or more frequency polygons may be drawn on the same diagram for comparison purposes without confusion, especially if different colours or different methods of drawing (eg continuous, dotted etc) are used.

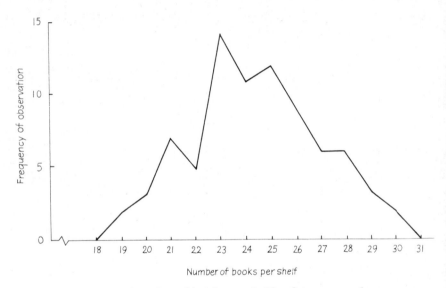

Figure 1.8: Number of books per shelf — frequency polygon

Cumulative frequency
In certain situations, the raw data may usefully be manipulated in a different way. For example, an investigation of an abstracts bulletin to determine time lags between publication of the original documents and publication of the abstracts yielded the raw data in the frequency table of Figure 1.9.

22

Time lag (months)	1	2	3	4	5
Number of abstracts	5	16	29	5	4

Figure 1.9: Time lag of abstracts – frequency table

From these figures, the relative frequencies may be determined to show what proportion of all the abstracts in the volume have a time lag of so many months (Figure 1.10).

Time lag (months)	Relative frequency
1	0.085
2	0.271
3	0.491
4	0.085
5	0.068

Figure 1.10: Time lag of abstracts
– relative frequencies

Thus, 0.492 (or almost half) of the abstracts in the volume exhibited a time lag of three months.

However, it could be of interest to know the total number of abstracts or, alternatively, the proportion of all the abstracts that have a time lag equal to or less than a specified figure. This is a problem of determining the *cumulative frequency*. For example, the number of abstracts with a time lag of three months or less will be 5 + 16 + 29. Figure 1.11 shows the full table of cumulative frequencies and relative cumulative frequencies. It can be seen that 21 of the abstracts – or 0.356 of the total number of abstracts – had a time lag of 2 months or less.

The data from Figure 1.11 can be shown graphically in a *cumulative frequency graph* (Figure 1.12). Note that these data relate to abstracts of monthly periodicals and that the variable quantity of time lag increases in integral steps of one month. The graph is therefore drawn in integral steps. To join the points by straight lines or by a curve would imply time lags of parts of months – which would be patently wrong.

However, for some data, it would be correct to join the points and

23

Time lag (months)	Cumulative frequency	Relative cumulative frequency
1	5	0.085
2	21	0.356
3	50	0.847
4	55	0.932
5	59	1.000

Figure 1.11: Time lag of abstracts – cumulative frequencies

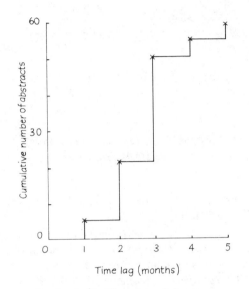

Figure 1.12: Time lag of abstracts
– cumulative frequency graph

incorrect to draw the graph in steps. An investigation of the length (in words) of abstracts yielded the data in Figure 1.13. To have shown increments in length of only one word would have created a very long table with a very large number of very small steps in the cumulative number of abstracts. On the other hand, it would not be correct to show steps only for the lengths 25, 30, 35 etc given in the table since there could be abstracts of actual length, say, 26 words or 27 words and so on. Therefore, the cumulative frequency graph is drawn as a continuous curve as in Figure 1.14.

24

Length of abstract (L)	Number of abstracts of length L or less	Length of abstract (L)	Number of abstracts of length L or less
25	0	90	167
30	3	95	184
35	4	100	202
40	9	105	208
45	20	110	218
50	32	115	230
55	42	120	238
60	58	125	239
65	77	130	242
70	99	135	244
75	119	140	248
80	137	145	248
85	154	150	250

*Figure 1.13: Length of abstracts in **Economics abstracts**, July 1972 – cumulative frequency*

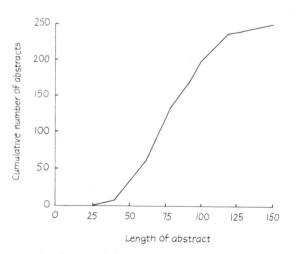

*Figure 1.14: Length of abstracts in **Economics abstracts**, July 1972 – cumulative frequency graph*

25

Grouped frequency

Ideally, all observations to be recorded in a histogram should be contained in between 10 and 25 columns. If the number of possible values of the variable exceeds this number, it is necessary to sort the observations into a series of groups containing consecutive values of the variable and to count the number of observations in each group.

For example, the data relating to the length of abstracts referred to in the previous section includes 250 observations with very many different lengths, the shortest containing only 28 words and the longest 148 words. If these abstracts are arranged in groups, with each group containing a range of lengths of 5 words, there will be 25 groups as shown in the *grouped frequency table* of Figure 1.15.

Length of abstract (Number of words)	Number of abstracts	Length of abstract (Number of words)	Number of abstracts
26-30	3	86-90	13
31-35	1	91-95	17
36-40	5	96-100	18
41-45	11	101-105	6
46-50	12	106-110	10
51-55	10	111-115	12
56-60	16	116-120	8
61-65	19	121-125	1
66-70	22	126-130	3
71-75	20	131-135	2
76-80	18	136-140	4
81-85	17	141-145	0
		146-150	2

*Figure 1.15: Length of abstracts in **Economics abstracts**, July 1972 – grouped frequency (group width = 5 words)*

The number of groups could be reduced by extending the range of values included within each group. If, with the data on length of abstract, a group is given a width of 10 words instead of 5 words, the tabulation now appears as in Figure 1.16.

26

Length of abstract (Number of words)	Number of abstracts	Length of abstract (Number of words)	Number of abstracts
26-35	4	86-95	30
36-45	16	96-105	24
46-55	22	106-115	22
56-65	35	116-125	9
66-75	42	126-135	5
76-85	35	136-145	4
		146-155	2

*Figure 1.16: Length of abstracts in **Economics abstracts**, July 1972 – grouped frequency (group width = 10 words)*

By careful choice of group width, the distribution of the observations may be brought out to best advantage. Thus, Figure 1.16 shows quite distinctly that there are comparatively few short abstracts or long abstracts and a prominent peak of abstracts with a length in the region of 66-75 words. The latter feature is not obvious from Figure 1.15.

Diagrammatically, grouped data can be presented either as a histogram (Figure 1.17) or a frequency polygon.

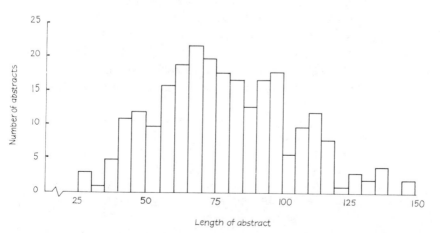

*Figure 1.17: Lengths of abstracts in **Economics abstracts**, July 1972*

27

Care must also be taken in defining groups. It would not be possible to use groups of 25-30, 30-35, 35-40 etc for the lengths of abstracts since a 30-word abstract would belong to more than one group. Hence, the reason for defining the groups as 26-30, 31-35, 36-40 etc will be clear. Of course, if half-words were possible, this latter grouping would be unacceptable since there would be no group into which $30\frac{1}{2}$ could be placed. In such a situation, appropriate grouping would be $25\frac{1}{4}$-$30\frac{1}{4}$, $30\frac{1}{4}$-$35\frac{1}{4}$, $35\frac{1}{4}$-$40\frac{1}{4}$ etc.

Examples

1.1 For the data in Figure 1.16, draw (a) a histogram (b) a frequency polygon.

1.2 For the data in Figure 1.4, draw a cumulative frequency graph.

1.3 Draw histograms, frequency polygons, and cumulative frequency graphs to represent the data in the following three examples:

(a) The number of index terms used to describe each of 72 periodical articles is given by:

No of index terms	1	2	3	4	5	6	7	8	9	10	11	12	13	14
Number of articles	0	0	5	8	12	7	9	9	10	5	3	2	1	1

(b) The heights of a collection of books are as follows:

Height (inches)	$5\frac{1}{2}$	6	$6\frac{1}{2}$	7	$7\frac{1}{2}$	8	$8\frac{1}{2}$	9	$9\frac{1}{2}$	10	$10\frac{1}{2}$	11
Number of books	1	0	3	4	4	2	4	5	2	2	2	1

(c) A count of the number of words per line on the page of a book yielded the following data:

Number of words/line	4	5	8	9	10	11	12	13	14	15	16	17
Number of lines	1	1	2	3	2	7	11	14	3	2	1	1

1.4 Collect similar data to that contained in examples 1.3(b) and 1.3(c) and superimpose on the frequency polygons for those data.

1.5 Draw appropriate diagrams to represent the following data which are the daily issues of junior books from a public library:

76	16	61	37	54	58	23	19	46	38	16	45
84	58	50	30	61	30	47	27	17	42	44	25
38	18	10	29	50	10	36	70	45	58	50	29
26	50	31	44	54	24	34	52	20	58	59	38
21	38	54	38	54	16	37	29	30	38	22	6

1.6 Draw appropriate diagrams to represent the following data which are the prices of volumes advertised in a publisher's list in 1981:

19.95	10.50	25.00	30.00	30.00	15.00	25.00
9.95	9.95	30.00	30.00	12.00	14.50	25.00
27.50	30.00	16.00	30.00	22.50	27.50	18.00
12.50	32.50	18.00	17.50	32.50	21.00	45.00
21.00	9.95	35.00	25.00	17.00	21.00	12.50
35.00	32.50	12.00	9.50	32.50	17.00	30.00
15.00	35.00	15.00	9.95	27.50	35.00	21.50
17.50	20.00	22.00	17.50	28.00	7.50	20.00
15.00	35.00	45.00	19.50	30.00	21.00	16.00
12.00	24.00	7.50	18.50	24.00	12.00	30.00
25.00	27.50	45.00	17.00	55.00	37.50	3.50
8.00	37.50	40.00	20.50	12.00	24.00	12.50
5.95	30.00	15.00	18.00	55.00	35.00	40.00
27.50	15.00	20.00	20.00	25.00	22.50	27.50

Chapter 2

AVERAGES

In a description of a large National Library, it was said that the *average* time taken to obtain a book in response to a reader's request was 40 minutes and that it may be obtained in as little as 2 minutes. On the other hand, in some cases, the book requested could not be traced at all. That description conveyed the impression that was presumably intended, namely that most readers making a request could expect to have a wait of about forty minutes. If they were lucky, they may have to wait only two minutes: if they were unlucky, they may never receive what they asked for.

The *average* is a simple way of conveying information about a number of observations of a quantitative variable.

However, the statement and deduction in the first paragraph are imprecise since, in statistical terms, there are three common measures of 'average', the *mode*, the *median* and the *mean*. The above situation can be used to illustrate the various possibilities according to which average is assumed.

Mode

If the 'average' were the mode, it would mean that a 40 minute delay would be experienced more often than a delay of any other length of time. Let us suppose that the statement was based on only eleven observations, in which case the actual delays experienced by the eleven readers might be:

$$2 \quad 20 \quad 30 \quad 40 \quad 40 \quad 40 \quad 40 \quad 40 \quad 40 \quad 40 \quad 42$$

In this sample, a majority of the observations have the modal delay of 40 minutes, whilst only three have a delay less than the mode.

The mode would also be 40 if the observations were:

$$2 \quad 2 \quad 3 \quad 3 \quad 4 \quad 4 \quad 5 \quad 40 \quad 40 \quad 40 \quad 42$$

In this sample, only a few of the observations have the modal delay, whilst the majority have a delay less than the mode.

On the other hand, the mode would also be 40 if the observations were:

2 40 40 40 100 200 300 400 500 600 700

Again, only a few of the observations have the modal value, whilst the majority have a delay far in excess of the mode.

The original statement was probably meant to imply a situation similar to the first sample, in which case a reader would be resigned to waiting for 40 minutes, would not notice an occasional delay of two minutes longer and would be delighted in a few instances that the delay was appreciably shorter.

However, the other two situations would fit the description and, in both cases, the reader might wonder at having been mislead since, in the former, there is a high chance that the delay is only a matter of minutes whereas, in the latter, there is a high chance that he would be waiting for hours.

Thus, the mode is a measure of average to the extent that it is that value of the variable that occurs most frequently, but it is not a very precise representation of all the observations. This does not mean to say that the mode is necessarily an unsatisfactory measure of average. It is easy to find and, in some circumstances, it gives quite an adequate measure of average. For example, if the general pattern of time delay in obtaining books is similar in different libraries, the mode is a quickly determined estimate that can be used to compare the delays that might be expected in the libraries concerned. Suppose that figures for the two libraries are:

| Library A | 2 | 20 | 30 | 40 | 40 | 40 | 40 | 40 | 40 | 40 | 42 |
| Library B | 2 | 4 | 7 | 10 | 10 | 10 | 10 | 10 | 10 | 10 | 15 |

There is little doubt that Library B would be preferred to Library A and that is reflected in the fact that the modal delay for Library B is only 10 minutes whilst the modal delay for Library A is 40 minutes.

Median

Returning now to the situation in the National Library described in the first paragraph, if the statement had meant that the median time taken to obtain a book was 40 minutes, the interpretation would be different from that for the mode but perhaps would not be any more helpful. All that it would imply would be that the expected delay would be 40 minutes or less on as many occasions as it would be 40 minutes or more. A delay of exactly 40 minutes is not necessarily such a common occurrence as with the mode but, for better or for worse, the odds are more favourably spread between a short wait and a long wait. We would know that, out of eleven observations, five would be of 40 minutes or less and five would be of 40 minutes or more. But how much less and how much more, we cannot tell. The waiting times might be quite attractive:

$$2 \quad 3 \quad 4 \quad 5 \quad 6 \quad 40 \quad 41 \quad 42 \quad 43 \quad 44 \quad 45$$

or they might be quite unattractive:

$$2 \quad 36 \quad 37 \quad 38 \quad 39 \quad 40 \quad 100 \quad 200 \quad 300 \quad 400 \quad 500$$

In fact, the time delays in excess of 40 could each be ten times as long without affecting the statement that the median time is 40 minutes. In other words, so long as the median is quoted as the 'middle figure', the actual magnitudes of the other observations do not affect the situation.

So, like the mode, the median is of restricted use but, also like the mode, the median can be valuable in certain circumstances. It is commonly used to indicate the average salary of a body of people and enables an individual to determine whether he/she is in that half of the population with a greater or less than average salary. Thus, if a librarian's median salary were £6,500, an individual librarian may be pleased to note that he is earning £7,000 − although he has no idea whether top salaries are of the order of £10,000 or £20,000.

Mean

Whilst neither the mode nor the median reflects the actual values of all the other observations, that is not true of the mean. It is the arithmetic mean that is, in fact, usually meant when an 'average' is referred to without qualification. The mean is found by adding together the magnitudes of all the observations and then dividing by the number of observations. The mean therefore gives due weight to all the observations, although the mean itself may not actually have been observed. For example, the mean time delay of 40 minutes would be calculated from the following observations:

$$2 \quad 12 \quad 22 \quad 32 \quad 45 \quad 47 \quad 50 \quad 53 \quad 56 \quad 59 \quad 62$$

Nor is the number of observations with magnitudes less than the mean necessarily equal to the number of observations with magnitude greater than the mean (cf median). In the above sample, there are fewer observations less than 40 than there are observations more than 40. In the following sample, the reverse is true, although the mean is again 40:

$$2 \quad 7 \quad 12 \quad 17 \quad 22 \quad 27 \quad 32 \quad 37 \quad 89 \quad 95 \quad 100$$

All that can be said of the mean therefore is that it is a figure representative of the magnitudes of all the observations of a quantitative variable and which can be used with some confidence for further mathematical calculations. Faith must, of course, be put in the discretion of the person who has deduced the mean. The following is an extreme case which would still produce a mean value of 40:

$$2 \quad 2 \quad 2 \quad 2 \quad 2 \quad 2 \quad 2 \quad 2 \quad 2 \quad 2 \quad 420$$

However, for some purposes, it would be sensible to discard the 420 as being completely unrepresentative and to deduce the mean to be 2. Although the reader would be very unhappy to have to wait for a book on one occasion for seven hours, he would prefer to know that he would have only 2 minutes to wait on every other occasion, rather than be told that the average waiting time would be 40 minutes. The desired result would, of course, be achieved by quoting the median (ie 2) as the average quantity, thereby ignoring the magnitude of the one very high value which the mean takes into consideration.

On the other hand, if, for any reason, the librarian wished to deduce from the mean the total time wasted by readers, assumption that the mean is 2 would lead to an erroneous result. If the average were taken as 2, it would be deduced that eleven readers would waste a total of only 22 minutes, whereas, if the average is taken as 40 (taking the value of 420 into consideration), the eleven readers would waste a total of 440 minutes — which a summation of the figures given in the last sample above shows to be correct. For such a deduction, the mean — based on all observations — is the average that must be used, not the median and not the mode.

The conclusion to be drawn from the preceding discussion is that all three forms of average have their uses but care must be taken to choose the right average in any particular situation and to interpret it with care.

Finding the average

When there is only a small number of observations, the data can be put in the form of an array from which the mode can be spotted by inspection. For example, the following figures are the number of entries in an index for each of thirteen documents:

$$2 \quad 4 \quad 3 \quad 5 \quad 4 \quad 5 \quad 5 \quad 3 \quad 6 \quad 4 \quad 3 \quad 5 \quad 6$$

In an array, the figures are:

$$2 \quad 3 \quad 3 \quad 3 \quad 4 \quad 4 \quad 4 \quad 5 \quad 5 \quad 5 \quad 5 \quad 6 \quad 6$$

An inspection shows that the figure 5 occurs four times, the figures 3 and 4 each occur three times, figure 6 appears twice and figure 2 occurs only once. Thus 5 is that value of the variable (the number of index entries per document) that occurs most frequently and therefore the mode is 5.

The mode can be determined from a histogram or from a frequency polygon by reading the value of the variable on the horizontal axis corresponding to the highest point of the diagram (ie 23 in Figures 1.6 and 1.8).

It is possible for a set of data to display more than one mode. In the array

$$2 \quad 3 \quad 3 \quad 3 \quad 3 \quad 4 \quad 4 \quad 4 \quad 5 \quad 5 \quad 5 \quad 5 \quad 6 \quad 6$$

there is a mode at 3 as well as at 5 and the data are said to be bi-modal.

To find the median, it is essential for the data to be put in an array. The array is divided into two halves, in which case, with the data from the last paragraph, we get six observations in each half and one left over in the middle:

$$2 \quad 3 \quad 3 \quad 3 \quad 4 \quad 4 \qquad 4 \qquad 5 \quad 5 \quad 5 \quad 5 \quad 6 \quad 6$$

This middle value is the median, viz 4. There are as many observations greater in magnitude or equal to the median as there are observations less in magnitude or equal to the median.

If there were an even number of observations in the array, there would be no middle value as such:

$$2 \quad 3 \quad 3 \quad 3 \quad 4 \quad 4 \qquad 5 \quad 5 \quad 5 \quad 5 \quad 6 \quad 6 \quad 7$$

The median is then found by adding the two figures bordering on the middle and dividing their sum by two, ie the median is $4\frac{1}{2}$. Note that, whereas the mode is necessarily one of the observed values, the median may not be.

34

The mean is found by adding together all the observed values of the variable and dividing their sum by the total number of observations, thus:

$$\frac{2 + 3 + 3 + 3 + 4 + 4 + 4 + 5 + 5 + 5 + 5 + 6}{12}$$

$$= \tfrac{49}{12}$$

$$= 4.083$$

Again, note that the mean is not necessarily one of the observed values of the variable.

It is much easier to indicate how to find the mean by expressing the procedure algebraically. The letter x is used to represent any value of the variable. So, in the above example, x represents the magnitude of any of the twelve observations. The Greek capital letter sigma (Σ) is used to indicate the requirement to add together. So, Σx specifies that all the possible values of x are to be added together, thus:

$$\Sigma x = 2 + 3 + 3 + 3 + 4 + 4 + 4 + 5 + 5 + 5 + 5 + 6$$

The letter N is used to represent the number of observations — twelve in the above example. The Greek letter mu (μ) is used to represent the mean.

Then we can write the equation:

$$\mu = \frac{\Sigma x}{N}$$

When there is a large number of observations, the data are more satisfactorily recorded in the form of a frequency table. Figure 2.1 gives the number of entries in an index for each of 250 documents.

No of index entries	0	1	2	3	4	5	6	7	8	9	10	11	12	13	14	15	16
No of documents	0	16	39	65	49	29	12	17	10	5	3	2	0	0	1	0	2

Figure 2.1: Frequency table showing number of index entries for a collection of documents

Note that, in this table, the data are already in an array, the variable being the 'Number of index entries' and the number of observations being the 'Number of documents'. Thus, there are, for example, 39 observations of documents having two index entries each.

35

To find the median, first of all total the number of observations by adding together the numbers of documents in each group, ie

$$0 + 16 + 39 + 65 + 49 + 29 + 12 + 17 + 10 + 5 + 3$$
$$+ 2 + 0 + 0 + 1 + 0 + 2 = 250$$

The middle of the array will therefore be between the 125th and 126th observations. By starting at the left hand side and totalling the number of observations until the 125th observation is reached —

$$0 + 16 + 39 + 65 + 5 = 125$$

— the 125th and 126th observations in the array are found to be the 5th and 6th observations in the group of 49 documents in the frequency table. Reading the values of the variable corresponding to these two observations, it will be found that both documents had four index entries. Hence the median is 4.

To find the mean, it must be appreciated that the total number of index entries will be found by multiplying each value of the variable by the number of times it was observed. Thus, for the 39 documents which each had two index entries, the total number of index entries will be 2 multiplied by 39. The total number of index entries for all the documents will therefore be:

$$(1 \times 16) + (2 \times 39) + (3 \times 65) + (4 \times 49)$$
$$+ (5 \times 29) + (6 \times 12) \ldots + (16 \times 2)$$

This is Σx.

The total number of observations is, in this example, the total number of documents and that is found by adding together the figures in that row of the table:

$$16 + 39 + 65 + 49 + 29 + 12 + 17 + 10 + 5 + 3 + 2 + 1 + 2$$

This is N.

The mean μ is therefore given by the expression:

$$\frac{\Sigma x}{N} = \frac{(1 \times 16) + (2 \times 39) + (3 \times 65) + (4 \times 49) \ldots + (16 \times 2)}{16 + 39 + 65 + 49 \ldots + 2}$$

$$= \frac{16 + 78 + 195 + 196 \ldots + 32}{250}$$

$$= \frac{1044}{250}$$

$$= 4.176$$

It will be noted that the few exceptionally large values of the variable have caused the value of the mean to be somewhat higher than the median.

If the data are grouped, as in Figure 1.16, the situation is a little more complicated. In that case, the variable is the 'Length of abstract' and the number of observations is the 'Number of abstracts' and the data are presented as an array as shown in Figure 1.16.

The mode is found by inspecting the number of observations to find the largest figure — which is 42. The value of the variable corresponding to that group of observations is 66-75, so the modal length of abstract is 66-75 words.

To find the median, the total number of abstracts is found by adding:

$$4 + 16 + 22 + 35 \ldots + 4 + 2$$

which comes to 250.

The middle of the array is therefore approximately the 125th observation. Totalling from the end of the array until the 125th observation is reached —

$$4 + 16 + 22 + 35 + 42 + 6$$

— it will be found that the 125th observation is the 6th in the group of 35 for which the length of abstract is 76-85 words. Since the median is the 6th observation out of 35 in the group with a range of ten words, it is found by adding $\frac{6}{35} \times 10$ to the boundary of the group. Since the last value in the preceding group is 75 and the first value in the group in question is 76, the boundary will be 75.5. Hence the median is taken as:

$$75.5 + \tfrac{6}{35} \times 10 = 75.5 + 1.71$$

$$= 77.21$$

In calculating the mean, it is assumed that the value of the variable for each group is the mid-point of the group. For example, for the group with length of abstracts of 76-85 words, the value of the variable is taken as 80.5 — found by adding 76 and 85 and dividing the sum by 2. Figure 1.16 can then be re-tabulated as shown in Figure 2.2. The mean can now be found in exactly the same way as it is from a frequency table, ie:

$$\mu = \frac{(30.5 \times 4) + (40.5 \times 16) + (50.5 \times 22) \ldots + (150.5 \times 2)}{4 + 16 + 22 \ldots + 2}$$

$$= \frac{19935}{250}$$

$$= 79.74$$

Length of abstract (Group mid-point)	Number of abstracts	Length of abstract (Group mid-point)	Number of abstracts
30.5	4	90.5	30
40.5	16	100.5	24
50.5	22	110.5	22
60.5	35	120.5	9
70.5	42	130.5	5
80.5	35	140.5	4
		150.5	2

Figure 2.2: Length of abstracts in **Economics abstracts**, *July 1972, showing mid-points of groups*

Examples

For each of the following sets of data, determine:

(a) the mode (b) the median (c) the mean

2.1 Fifteen items were placed on set-text in a library and the number of times that each was used was noted as:

20 15 21 19 20 17 21 22 18 19 20 20 23 20 18

2.2 In studying the use of periodical literature, the number of borrowings of back issues was investigated with the following results:

Age of issue (months)	1	2	3	4	5	6	7	8	9	10	11	12
No of borrowings	3	5	8	6	6	4	3	2	2	1	1	1

2.3 When a number of readers were asked how many different periodicals they read quarterly, the response was:

No of periodicals read	0	1	2	3	4	5	6	7
No of readers	5	12	17	15	12	7	5	2

2.4 The costs of a collection of paperbacks were as follows:

Cost per book (pence)	40	45	50	55	60	65	70	75	80	85
Number of books	1	3	3	7	10	13	6	4	2	1

2.5 The weekly issues of fiction books in a public library over a period of time were:

Number of weekly issues	Number of weeks	Number of weekly issues	Number of weeks
51-60	1	151-160	13
61-70	5	161-170	12
71-80	5	171-180	8
81-90	15	181-190	8
91-100	19	191-200	4
101-110	30	201-210	3
111-120	35	211-220	2
121-130	25	221-230	1
131-140	21	231-240	1
141-150	17		

2.6 For the data in examples 1.5 and 1.6, draw up grouped frequency tables and determine the mode, median and mean in each case.

Chapter 3

DISPERSION

Histograms and frequency polygons show how the observations of different values of a variable quantity are distributed. They are graphical presentations of *frequency distributions* — showing the frequency of observation of each value of the variable. If there were a very large number of observations of a large number of values of a variable, the angular graphs would approximate more and more closely to a smooth curve. A commonly occurring curve representing collections of data is the *normal distribution*. This is a smooth, symmetrical, bell-shaped curve and is illustrated in Figure 3.1.

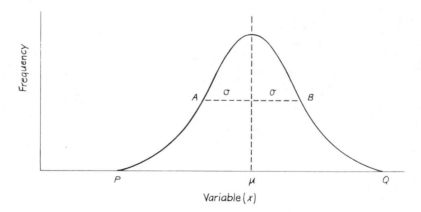

Figure 3.1: A normal distribution

The mean of the normal distribution (μ) is that point on the horizontal axis midway between points P and Q where the curve cuts the axis. Thus, the mean determines the position of the distribution on the horizontal axis of the diagram. Whilst that is useful information, it is

40

insufficient to describe the other features of the distribution. Referring to the problem of waiting time in a library discussed in Chapter 2, to quote the mean waiting time as 40 minutes conveys some helpful impression to readers but they have no idea whether the actual waiting times are likely to range between, say, 35 minutes and 45 minutes or between 2 minutes and 78 minutes. It is necessary, therefore, to specify the spread of the distribution in order to indicate the *dispersion* of the variable.

Range
An easy way to indicate dispersion is to quote the range, that is the difference between the values of the variable at points P and Q (Figure 3.1). However, in practice, the extreme values of data may be unrepresentative of the distribution and they would give an inaccurate impression of the dispersion. An example of that problem is seen in Figure 2.1 where the few observations of 14 and 16 index entries makes the range much greater than it effectively is.

Standard deviation
A more difficult, but much more satisfactory, method of measuring the dispersion is to utilize the points of inflection. These are the points where the central convex part of the normal distribution curve joins the outer concave parts. These points are labelled A and B in Figure 3.1. The distance of point A or point B from the line of symmetry (at μ) is known as the *standard deviation* and is represented by the Greek letter little sigma σ. The square of the standard deviation (ie σ^2) is known as the *variance*.

By specifying the standard deviation, it is possible to differentiate between normal distributions of different dispersions. Figure 3.2 shows two normal distribution curves, labelled 1 and 2, with means μ_1 and μ_2 and standard deviations σ_1 and σ_2 respectively.

Thus, by specifying the mean and the standard deviation, it is made clear where on the horizontal axis the normal distribution is located and how great its dispersion is.

A feature of a normal distribution is that the range is approximately six times the standard deviation. Hence, in Figure 3.1, PQ is approximately equal to 6σ.

A further feature is that the number of observations in the distribution is represented by the area under the curve. In addition, it is known that the area under that part of the curve within one standard deviation

41

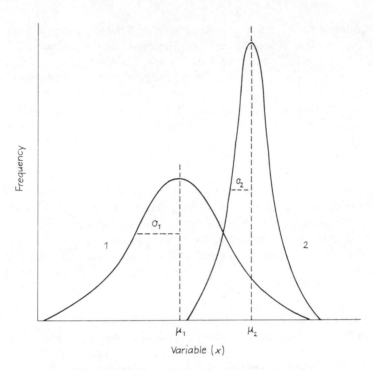

Figure 3.2: Normal distribution curves with different dispersions

from the mean (ie the shaded part of Figure 3.3) is 68.3% of the whole area under the curve. Therefore, 68.3% of all observations are within one standard deviation from the mean.

The area under that part of the curve within twice the standard deviation from the mean is 95.4% of the whole area and therefore 95.4% of all observations are within two standard deviations from the mean.

Therefore, the number of observations which lie outside two standard deviations from the mean are 4.6% of the whole, 2.3% being on the lower end and 2.3% being on the higher end of the distribution.

It will be clear that the standard deviation is an important measure for defining the dispersion of the variable in a normal distribution. The practical value of a knowledge of the standard deviation can be illustrated with reference to the example relating to the time taken to obtain a book in a library which was introduced in Chapter 2. If a reader

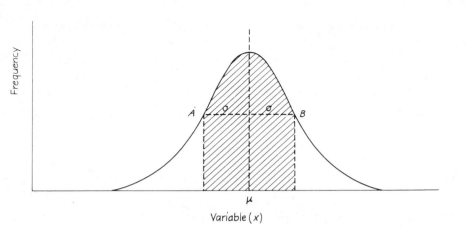

*Figure 3.3: Normal distribution marking boundaries
one standard deviation from the mean*

complained to the librarian that he had to wait longer than the average of all other readers for a book to be brought to him, does the librarian take any serious notice? 'How much longer?' he may well ask, to which the answer may be 'Well, I waited 50 minutes whereas the mean waiting time is only 40 minutes'. Without a knowledge of the dispersion, the librarian would not know whether many people have to wait even longer or only a few, if any. If the standard deviation were 5 minutes, there may be some cause for complaint because less than 2.3% (ie 100 − 95.4/2) of readers could be expected to have to wait more than 50 minutes (ie the mean plus twice the standard deviation). If, on the other hand, the standard deviation were 10 minutes, the librarian would commiserate but declare that at least 15% (ie 100 − 68.3/2) could be expected to have to wait 50 minutes or more (ie the mean plus one standard deviation).

Finding the standard deviation
Step 1: Determine the mean (μ) as described in Chapter 2.
Step 2: Determine the difference between each value of the variable (x) and the mean (μ). This is known as the *deviation* $(x - \mu)$.
Step 3: Square each value of the deviation, ie $(x - \mu)^2$.
Step 4: Add together the various values of $(x - \mu)^2$, ie $\Sigma(x - \mu)^2$.
Step 5: Divide the answer to Step 4 by the number of observations (N).
Step 6: Take the square root of the answer to Step 5.

Thus, putting Steps 2-6 together, the standard deviation is given by:

$$\sigma = \sqrt{\frac{\Sigma(x - \mu)^2}{N}}$$

If this procedure is applied to a set of observations – 1, 2, 3, 4, and 5:

Step 1:

$$\mu = \frac{\Sigma x}{N}$$

$$= \frac{1 + 2 + 3 + 4 + 5}{5}$$

$$= 3$$

Steps 2-4:

x	$(x - \mu)$	$(x - \mu)^2$
1	-2	4
2	-1	1
3	0	0
4	$+1$	1
5	$+2$	4
	$\Sigma(x - \mu)^2 =$	10

Step 5:

$$\frac{\Sigma(x - \mu)^2}{N} = \frac{10}{5}$$

$$= 2$$

Step 6:

$$\sigma = \sqrt{\frac{\Sigma(x - \mu)^2}{N}}$$

$$= \sqrt{2}$$

$$= 1.414$$

If there is a large number of observations, the calculation of the standard deviation using the above formula can be tedious, especially if the computed value of the mean (μ) is fractional. The problem can be simplified by rearranging the expression to the form:

44

$$\sigma = \sqrt{\frac{\Sigma x^2}{N} - \mu^2}$$

Using the same set of observations, the calculation now becomes:

x	x^2
1	1
2	4
3	9
4	16
5	25
$\Sigma x^2 = $	55

$$\sigma = \sqrt{\frac{\Sigma x^2}{N} - \mu^2}$$

$$= \sqrt{\tfrac{55}{5} - 3^2}$$

$$= \sqrt{11 - 9}$$

$$= \sqrt{2}$$

$$= 1.414$$

When applying this procedure to data presented in a frequency table, in determining the value of Σx^2, each value of the variable (x) is squared and then multiplied by the number of times it was observed. Thus, using the data of Figure 2.1:

$$\Sigma x^2 = (1^2 \times 16) + (2^2 \times 39) + (3^2 \times 65) \ldots + (16^2 \times 2)$$

$$= 5826$$

$$N = 250$$

$$\mu = 4.176 \ \text{(see p36)}$$

Therefore:

$$\sigma = \sqrt{\tfrac{5826}{250} - 4.176^2}$$

$$= \sqrt{23.304 - 17.439}$$

$$= \sqrt{5.865}$$

$$= 2.422$$

The formula can be applied in a similar fashion to grouped data, as, for example, the data in Figure 1.15. In this case, the values of x are taken as the mean values for each group, eg the value of x for the group 61-65 is 63.

Then:

$N = 250$

$$\mu = \frac{(28 \times 3) + (33 \times 1) + (38 \times 5) + (43 \times 11) \ldots + (148 \times 2)}{3 + 1 + 5 + 11 \ldots + 2}$$

$$= \frac{19890}{250}$$

$$= 79.56$$

$$\sigma = \sqrt{\frac{(28^2 \times 3) + (33^2 \times 1) + (38^2 \times 5) \ldots + (148^2 \times 2)}{250} - 79.56^2}$$

$$= \sqrt{\frac{1736040}{250} - 6329.79}$$

$$= \sqrt{6944.16 - 6329.79}$$

$$= \sqrt{614.37}$$

$$= 24.79$$

Interquartile range

When the median is being used as a measure of average, the dispersion is not measured by the standard deviation but by the *interquartile range*. It will be recalled that the median is found by dividing the array of observations into two equal parts, but two histograms may have the same median yet have quite different dispersions (see Figures 3.4 and 3.5).

The two distributions can be defined by determining the values of their *quartiles*, ie those values of the variable above which 75% and 25% of the observations lie respectively. These positions are marked Q_1 and Q_2 on both figures, Q_1 being the *lower quartile* and Q_2 being the *upper quartile*. It will be apparent that, if the *interquartile range* $(Q_2 - Q_1)$ is specified, the shape of the distribution is defined.

Finding the interquartile range

The interquartile range for the distribution of number of books per shelf given in Figure 1.4 can be determined from the tabulated data or from the cumulative frequency graph.

From the tabulation, it will be apparent that, since there are 80

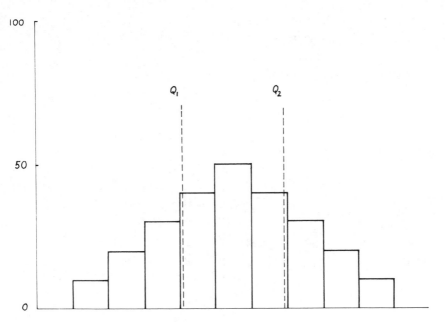

Figure 3.4: Histogram with large interquartile range

shelves altogether, the median lies between the 40th and 41st observation, ie the median is 24. Similarly, the lower quartile is between the 20th and 21st observation and is therefore 23 whilst the upper quartile is between the 60th and 61st observation and is therefore 26.

Hence, the interquartile range is $26 - 23$, ie 3. The *semi-interquartile range* – being half of the interquartile range – is often quoted and, in this example, is therefore $1\frac{1}{2}$.

A cumulative frequency graph for the data is given in Figure 3.6. By taking a horizontal line from the value 40 on the vertical axis until it meets the graph and dropping a perpendicular therefrom on to the horizontal axis, the value of the median can be read off as 24.

The quartiles can be found by drawing horizontal lines to the graph from the values of 20 and 60 on the vertical axis. Perpendiculars dropped from the graph to the horizontal axis show the values of the quartiles to be 23 and 26 respectively and the interquartile range to be 3. Note that the median is not necessarily mid way between the quartiles.

Other similar ranges may be specified to define the shape of the

47

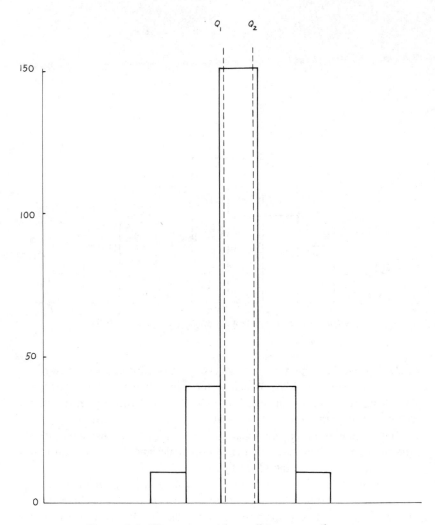

Figure 3.5: Histogram with small interquartile range

distribution more precisely. For example, the *decile range* measures the difference between the first decile (the point above which nine-tenths of the observations lie) and the ninth decile (the point above which one-tenth of the observations lie).

48

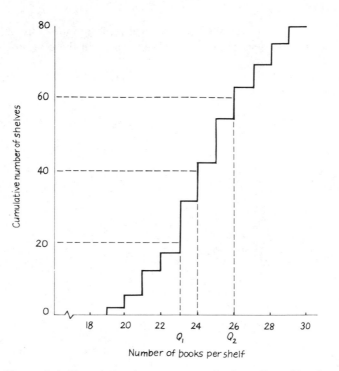

*Figure 3.6: Cumulative frequency graph of number of books
per shelf*

Skewness

Whilst the mean locates the position of a distribution on the horizontal
axis and the standard deviation defines the width of the distribution,
a third factor must be taken into consideration before the distribution
can be fully described. In practice, frequency distributions are not symmetrical but exhibit a certain measure of *skewness*, with the tail on one
side greater than the tail on the other. In a skew distribution, the
values of the mean, the mode and the median are different and the
relative values will depend on its precise shape. Various expressions
have been proposed to provide a measure of skewness, one being:

$$\frac{\text{Mean} - \text{Mode}}{\text{Standard deviation}}$$

In curve A of Figure 3.7, the mean is greater than the mode and
therefore the skewness is positive. In curve B, the mean is less than the

49

mode and therefore the skewness is negative. In a normal distribution, the mean and the mode are numerically equal and therefore the skewness is zero.

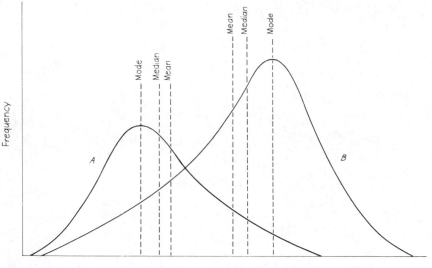

Figure 3.7: Skew distributions

In the distribution of Figure 2.1:

Mean = 4.176
Mode = 3.000
Standard deviation = 2.422

The degree of skewness of the distribution is therefore given by:

$$\frac{4.176 - 3.000}{2.422} = 0.486$$

The distribution of a number of index entries per document therefore displays a positive skewness with a tail to the right representing documents with comparatively high numbers of index entries.

An alternative expression for determining the degree of skewness that avoids the use of the less satisfactory mode is:

50

$$\frac{3 \times (\text{Mean} - \text{Median})}{\text{Standard deviation}}$$

The numerical value of the skewness is difficult to interpret but, as a rough guide, a value of +1 indicates that a distribution has a fairly high degree of positive skewness, ie a substantial tail to the right. Conversely, a distribution with a fairly high degree of negative skewness (with a substantial tail to the left) will have a skewness of magnitude in the region of −1. In a normal distribution, the mean and the mode coincide and therefore its skewness is zero in magnitude.

Otherwise, the numerical value of the skewness may be of use in comparing two or more distributions such as data on the number of index entries for documents in the physical sciences compared with data on the number of index entries for documents in the social sciences and/or the humanities.

Examples
Find the standard deviation, semi-interquartile range and degree of skewness for the data in examples 2.1 to 2.5 (pages 38-39).

Chapter 4

SAMPLING

In Chapters 2 and 3, it was assumed that observations were made on all possible occurrences of the variable, ie on an entire *population*. In this context, the word 'Population' refers to any group on which observations are made — not necessarily on persons but, for example, book issues, library shelves, online searches, and so on. In the worked examples, it was fortunate from the point of view of the amount of work involved that the populations were quite small. Basing calculations on observations of a whole population ensures accuracy of the result but, if the population is large, the processes of observation and calculation would be very long and tedious.

Therefore, in such circumstances, it is more economical to make use of only a part of the population and, in fact, this may be the only way of acquiring information about the whole population quickly and cheaply. That part of the population which is being investigated is known as the *sample*, the objective being to determine one or more characteristics (or *statistics*) of the sample from which information on the corresponding characteristics (or *parameters*) of the population can be deduced. A given population can give rise to many different samples from which statistical inferences about a whole population are to be drawn. If care is not taken, the sample may be biased, *bias* being a term used to describe how far the statistic of the sample lies from the parameter of the population. For example, if the purpose of the investigation were to determine the mean number of books contained on a library shelf, it would be unsatisfactory to take a sample of shelves entirely from the Law section of the library. The above-average thickness of the volumes of law reports would lead one to deduce that an average shelf will hold far fewer books than, in fact, is normally possible. It would also be unsatisfactory to take a sample that includes shelves on which only paperbacks are stored since they take up less than normal space and the sample could lead to a conclusion that an

52

average shelf will hold more books than, in fact, is normally possible. In both cases, the sample is biased and the consequences are seen in Figure 4.1 in which the distribution L represents the sample from the Law section and distribution P represents the sample from the paperback section.

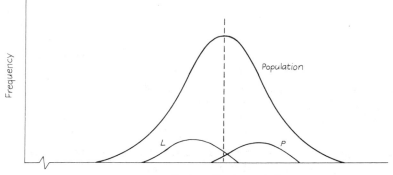

Figure 4.1: Distributions of the number of books per shelf in a whole library and in samples from the Law (L) and Paperback (P) sections

Bias can be minimized by choosing a *random sample*. In a random sample, each member of the population being investigated must have an equal chance of being included and therefore it is important that the population must be precisely defined before the sample is chosen. To assist in making a random selection, tables of random numbers are available (eg Lindley and Miller). The numbers in the tables have been arranged in an order free from bias and, by reading across lines or up or down columns from a randomly selected starting point, the numbers to be used for identifying observations to be selected from the population can be determined.

The 250 documents of the population tabulated in Figure 2.1 were numbered consecutively from 1 to 250 and two samples of ten documents were selected in accordance with random numbers from the tables, accepting any number of 250 or less from the table and rejecting any number in excess of 250. The number of index entries for each of the documents selected from the samples is recorded in Figure 4.2. Having selected the samples, the random observation numbers play no further part but, from the recorded data, statistics such as the mean and standard deviation can be calculated.

53

	SAMPLE 1		SAMPLE 2
Random observation number	*Number of index entries*	*Random observation number*	*Number of index entries*
201	3	161	9
221	6	10	4
162	5	102	2
45	5	142	2
36	2	78	2
17	3	129	4
202	2	28	4
87	1	87	1
57	2	230	3
116	3	130	2

Figure 4.2: Random samples of observations of the number of index entries relating to documents in a collection

The sample mean and standard deviation for Sample 1 are 3.2 and 1.62 respectively, and the sample mean and standard deviation for Sample 2 are 3.3 and 2.26 respectively. These statistics compare with the parameters of the population determined in Chapter 3, viz population mean 4.176 and population standard deviation 2.422.

The sample means appear to show a degree of bias when compared with the population mean. This is partly due to inherent bias, partly to the small size of samples and partly to the skewness of the population. The latter results in the value of its mean being rather inflated due to the small number of observations of exceptionally high value.

However, the important point to note is that the statistics vary from one sample to another and differ from the parameters of the population from which the samples are taken. In recognition of these differences between sample and population, different symbols are used to represent sample statistics from those used to represent population parameters. These are tabulated in Figure 4.3.

The expression for determining the mean of a sample is analogous to that for determining the mean of a population, viz:

$$\text{Sample mean } \bar{X} = \frac{\Sigma X}{n}$$

However, the expression for determining the standard deviation for a

	Parameter	Statistic
Value of variable	x	X
Number of observations	N	n
Mean	μ	$\overline{X}$
Standard deviation	σ	s

Figure 4.3: Symbols used to represent parameters and statistics

sample differs slightly in form from that for the population standard deviation so as to correct for bias inherent in the sampling process. Hence:

$$\text{Sample standard deviation } s = \sqrt{\frac{\Sigma(X - \overline{X})^2}{n - 1}}$$

In practice, it can be helpful to use a rearranged form of this expression, viz:

$$s = \sqrt{\frac{\Sigma X^2 - n\overline{X}^2}{n - 1}}$$

Random sampling is not always possible or appropriate and there are other methods of sampling that may be considered.

1 The size of the population may not be known and therefore a random sample giving every member of the population an equal opportunity of being selected could not be found. This would be the situation if a librarian were interested in those readers who make use of (say) the local history collection. In that case, *cluster sampling* would be used in which all people who fit the description would be included in the sample.

2 Although the size of the population may be known, it would not be easy to select a random sample. If, for example, the type of document abstracted in a year's cumulation of *Chemical abstracts* were of interest, the easiest procedure to follow would be *systematic sampling* in which the first complete abstract on every (say) twentieth page would be selected.

3 The population may be made up of sub-groups which have distinct characteristics. For example, if 40% of the bookstock of a library is fiction and 60% is non-fiction and it is known that volumes of fiction are normally borrowed for shorter periods than volumes of non-fiction, it would not be appropriate to take a random sample of books in an

investigation of the average loan period. If a sample of 100 books is taken, 40 of them should be fiction selected at random from the fiction books borrowed and 60 of them should be non-fiction selected at random from the non-fiction books borrowed. This procedure of *stratified sampling* ensures that the aggregated sample is more truly representative of a population consisting of two or more sub-groups in which members are more closely related to each other than to the population as a whole.

A further factor to be considered in the sampling process is whether an observation selected for a sample is − or is not − available for selection again. If there were a hundred books on the shelves and ten were taken as a sample and not replaced, the nature of the population of books will have changed and such a population is known as a *finite population*. On the other hand, if ten books are taken from the hundred on the shelves but, after each one has been selected, it is returned to the shelf with the opportunity of being selected again, the nature of the population is unchanged by the sampling process. Such a population is known as an *infinite population* and it is on such a population that the theory of random sampling is based.

If samples are selected from an infinite population, with each item being replaced in the population before the next item is selected, virtually an infinite number of samples can be selected from the population.

Each sample will have a mean and standard deviation which are likely to be different from the means and standard deviations of other samples taken from the population. The sample mean varies from one sample to another and so it is another example of a variable quantity. As such, the means of all the samples taken from a population form a frequency distribution known as a *sampling distribution of the mean*. It should be appreciated that there is only one population, a virtually infinite number of samples taken from the population, and only one sampling distribution of the mean. These are illustrated in Figure 4.4, drawn on separate axes for clarity.

The mean of the sampling distribution is referred to as the mean value of the means − or the *grand mean* − and is identical to the mean of the population from which the samples are taken. If the samples are large, for which it is assumed that there are thirty or more observations, and if the skewness of the population is only moderate, the sampling distribution is approximately normal. Moreover, the standard deviation of the sampling distribution − known as the *standard error of the mean*

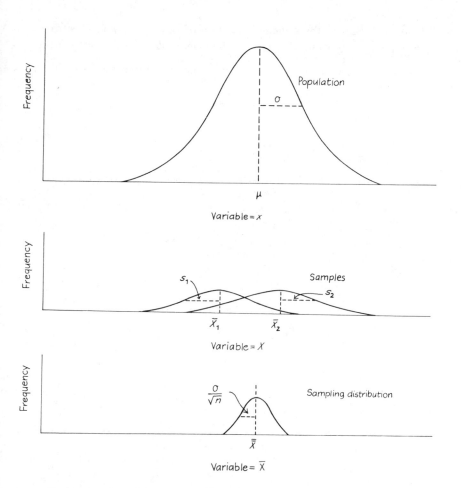

Figure 4.4: Frequency distributions for a population, samples taken from the population, and the sampling distribution of the mean

— is of magnitude $\dfrac{\sigma}{\sqrt{n}}$, which may be represented by the symbol $\sigma_{\bar{X}}$.

It must be appreciated that, in deriving the statistics, the mean value of the means is found from observations on samples but, in the last paragraph the standard error was defined in terms of the standard deviation of the population (σ). This information is not normally available — otherwise the whole point of sampling would be missed. However, the standard deviation of a sample (s) is a reasonably close

57

approximation to the standard deviation of the population. Therefore, in the absence of knowledge of σ, the magnitude of the standard error of the mean can be taken as $\dfrac{s}{\sqrt{n}}$, which may be represented by $s_{\bar{X}}$.

SAMPLE SIZE $n = 30$

Sample Number	Sample Mean $(\bar{X})$	Sample Standard Deviation (s)
1	4.97	3.00
2	3.97	2.01
3	4.13	3.22
4	4.23	2.95
5	4.23	2.31
6	4.60	3.15

$$\text{Mean value of the means} = 4.36$$
$$\text{Mean value of standard deviation} = 2.77$$
$$\text{Standard error} = \frac{2.77}{\sqrt{30}} = 0.51$$

SAMPLE SIZE $n = 60$

Sample Number	Sample Mean $(\bar{X})$	Sample Standard Deviation (s)
7	4.43	2.95
8	4.35	2.35
9	4.63	3.06
10	4.27	3.00
11	4.43	2.61
12	4.28	2.65

$$\text{Mean value of the means} = 4.40$$
$$\text{Mean value of standard deviation} = 2.77$$
$$\text{Standard error} = \frac{2.77}{\sqrt{60}} = 0.36$$

Figure 4.5: Data on number of index entries per document for two sizes of sample

In fact, s is a biased estimate of σ and applies only for large samples. For samples of less than thirty observations, an unbiased estimate is found from the expression:

$$\sigma = \sqrt{\frac{n}{n-1}} \times s$$

To illustrate the effect of increasing sample size, two groups of samples were taken from the data in Figure 2.1, one group with all samples containing thirty observations and the other group with all samples containing 60 observations. The data collected and deductions therefrom are set out in Figure 4.5.

The mean and standard deviation of the population are 4.176 and 2.427 respectively and the distribution of the population and the two sampling distributions of the mean are shown in Figure 4.6.

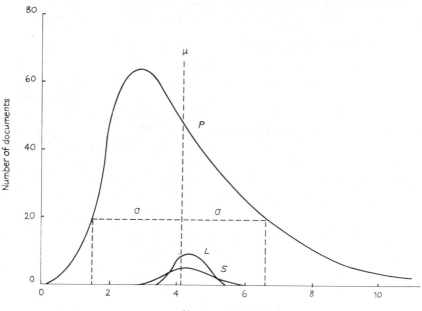

Figure 4.6: Frequency distribution of the population (P) and sampling distributions of the means of small samples (S) and large samples (L)

The points to note from this example are:

1 The mean value of the means of the random samples is close to

the mean of the population. (For an infinite number of samples, the mean value of the means is the same as the population mean.)

2   The standard deviations of the samples are reasonably close to the standard deviation of the population.

3   Doubling the sample size does not halve the standard error owing to the operation of square-rooting the value of n in calculating the standard error. In order to halve the standard error, the sample size would have to be quadrupled.

4   The distribution of the means of the large samples shows much less dispersion than that of the small samples.

An application of the last point relates to the degree of reproducibility or *precision* of results from various samples. It would be hoped that the statistics derived from several samples would be so similar to each other as to create confidence in their reliability. High precision is therefore obviously achieved by taking as large samples as possible. Thus high precision accompanies low dispersion, ie a low value of $\dfrac{\sigma}{\sqrt{n}}$ or $\dfrac{s}{\sqrt{n}}$. Consequently, the inverse of these fractions, viz $\dfrac{\sqrt{n}}{\sigma}$ or $\dfrac{\sqrt{n}}{s}$, can be used as measures of precision.

Whilst precision is affected by sample size, bias is not. If, in investigating the number of books stored on shelves in a library, the sample of shelves was taken entirely from the section containing law reports, it would not matter if the sample were doubled in size. All that would be achieved would be greater precision of the biased result, as shown in Figure 4.7.

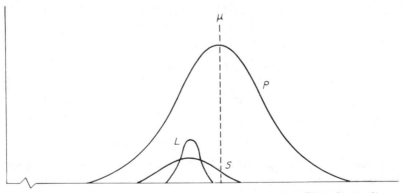

Figure 4.7: Frequency distribution of the population (P) and sampling distributions of the means of small samples (S) and large samples (L) both showing bias

Examples

4.1   A sample of 11 paperbacks was taken and their costs, in pence, were noted as:

          30 25 35 35 75 35 30 40 35 40 60

Calculate the standard deviation of the cost and the standard error of the mean.

4.2   From the Penguin *Dictionary of quotations*, three random samples, each containing five pages were taken. The mean numbers of quotations per page and the standard deviations for the three samples were:

Sample Number	Sample Mean	Sample Standard Deviation
1	29.8	3.34
2	32.0	2.83
3	24.0	4.53

Calculate (1) the mean value of the means (2) the mean value of the standard deviation and use that to find the standard error of the mean.

4.3   Number from 1 to 80 the items of data in Figure 1.2. Use a table of random numbers to select a sample of 20 shelves and determine the mean number of books per shelf and the standard deviation. Repeat for a number of other samples, each containing 20 shelves and hence determine the mean value of the means and the standard error of the mean. Repeat the exercise with 40 shelves in each sample and note the effect on the standard error of increasing the sample size.

4.4   Take a random sample of 30 items from a bibliography and note the time lag between the year of publication of each article referred to and the year of publication of the bibliography. Hence find the mean time lag and standard deviation for the sample. Repeat for a number of other samples each containing 30 items and then calculate the mean value of the means and the standard error of the mean.

4.5   By systematic sampling, take a sample of abstracts from an annual volume and note the length (in pages) of each article abstracted. Repeat for a number of other samples each including the same number of abstracts, and then calculate the mean value of the means and the standard error of the mean.

Chapter 5

STATISTICS AND PARAMETERS

One of the purposes of sampling and finding the statistics of samples is to obtain information about the population from which the samples have been taken. We wish to deduce the likely parameters of the population from the calculated statistics of the samples.

If an unbiased sample were taken from a population, it would be hoped that the sample mean would be a reasonable estimate of the population mean. Such an estimate is known as a *point estimate* but it is unlikely that the mean of a sample will be identical to the mean of the population.

As indicated in the last chapter, an infinite number of samples may be taken from an infinite population and the means of all the samples form the sampling distribution of the mean. It can, in fact, be shown that the mean of the sampling distribution (ie the grand mean) is identical to the population mean. However, it would not be practicable to take enough samples in order to find the exact value of the grand mean. The best that can be done is to take a finite number of samples and find the mean value of their means. The mean value of the means is likely to be closer to the population mean than a point estimate but we still cannot be certain that this procedure will give an exact estimate of the population mean. The likely difference between the mean value of the means so derived and the population mean will be indicated by the standard deviation of the sampling distribution. Hence, representing the mean value of the means of the samples by $\bar{\bar{X}}$, the population mean is likely to be between $\bar{\bar{X}} - \dfrac{s}{\sqrt{n}}$ and $\bar{\bar{X}} + \dfrac{s}{\sqrt{n}}$.

Although the effect of any extreme value of sample mean is minimized by basing the estimate of the population mean on a number of samples, the collection of data and performing the calculations for several samples is time-consuming and it would be helpful if an estimate of the population mean could be made from observations on a single

62

sample. This is, in fact, what a point estimate does — but some measure of the accuracy of the point estimate is required.

It must first be recalled from Chapter 3 that 95% of all observations in a normal distribution lie between two standard deviations below the mean and two standard deviations above the mean. Looked at from another point of view, any one observation can be expected, with 95% certainty, to lie between these limits. The points A and B in Figure 5.1 are therefore known as the 95% *confidence limits*.

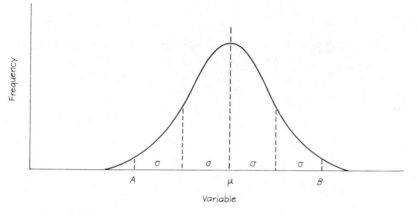

Figure 5.1: Normal distribution showing the 95% confidence limits (A and B)

Applying these principles to the sampling distribution of the mean, 95% of sample means lie between $(\mu - \frac{2\sigma}{\sqrt{n}})$ and $(\mu + \frac{2\sigma}{\sqrt{n}})$. Or, from the alternative point of view, any one sample mean can be expected, with 95 % certainty, to lie between these limits.

Hence:

$$\bar{X} > \mu - \frac{2\sigma}{\sqrt{n}}$$

$$\text{and } \bar{X} < \mu + \frac{2\sigma}{\sqrt{n}}$$

Rearranging these expressions:

$$\bar{X} + \frac{2\sigma}{\sqrt{n}} > \mu$$

$$\text{and } \bar{X} - \frac{2\sigma}{\sqrt{n}} < \mu$$

Now, combining these two expressions:

$$\bar{X} - \frac{2\sigma}{\sqrt{n}} < \mu < \bar{X} + \frac{2\sigma}{\sqrt{n}}$$

The values of $(\bar{X} - \frac{2\sigma}{\sqrt{n}})$ and $(\bar{X} + \frac{2\sigma}{\sqrt{n}})$ are the 95% confidence limits.

If the standard deviation of the population is not known, the standard deviation of the sample may be used as a reasonable approximation for samples containing at least 30 observations. Hence:

$$\bar{X} - \frac{2s}{\sqrt{n}} < \mu < \bar{X} + \frac{2s}{\sqrt{n}}$$

For smaller samples (ie samples containing less than 30 observations), s should be replaced by $s \sqrt{\frac{n}{n-1}}$.

Thus, from a knowledge of the mean and standard deviation of a single sample, the limits between which the population mean can be expected — with 95% confidence — to lie, can be determined.

Since the estimate of the population mean is based on observations of a single sample, every effort must be made to avoid bias if a satisfactory result is to be achieved.

Using the data for Sample 6 of Figure 4.5:

$$\bar{X} = 4.60$$
$$n = 30$$
$$s = 3.15$$

Therefore:

$$4.60 - \frac{2 \times 3.15}{\sqrt{30}} < \mu < 4.60 + \frac{2 \times 3.15}{\sqrt{30}}$$

$$3.45 < \mu < 5.75$$

Therefore, it can be stated with 95% confidence that μ lies between 3.45 and 5.75.

This compares with the value of 4.176 determined from a knowledge of the whole population (see Figure 2.1).

64

From the general expression for determining the limits of μ, it will be apparent that the larger the sample (ie the greater the value of n), the closer will be the estimate of μ. Thus, from Sample 12 of Figure 4.5:

$$\bar{X} = 4.28$$
$$n = 60$$
$$s = 2.65$$

Therefore:

$$4.28 - \frac{2 \times 2.65}{\sqrt{60}} < \mu < 4.28 + \frac{2 \times 2.65}{\sqrt{60}}$$

$$3.60 < \mu < 4.96$$

With the smaller sample, the difference between the limits is 2.30 whereas, with the larger sample, the difference is only 1.36.

Since the standard error involves the square root of the size of the sample rather than the size of the sample itself, the increase in sample size needed in order to narrow the limits must be correspondingly larger.

The size of the sample that should be taken can be determined if the closeness of the limits is specified and the standard deviation is known. The distance between the limits is $\frac{4s}{\sqrt{n}}$ and, if this distance is required to be (say) 0.75, it can be stated that:

$$\frac{4s}{\sqrt{n}} = 0.75$$

Hence:

$$\frac{4s}{0.75} = \sqrt{n}$$

Then:

$$n = \frac{16s^2}{0.75^2}$$

Taking the mean value of s for all the samples in Figure 4.5:

$$n = \frac{16 \times 2.77^2}{0.75^2}$$

$$= 218.25$$

So, to achieve the specified degree of accuracy, a sample containing about 218 observations would be necessary.

Examples

5.1 From the Penguin *Dictionary of quotations*, three random samples, each containing five pages were investigated. The mean number of quotations per page and the standard deviation for the three samples are as follows:

Sample	$\bar{X}$	s
1	29.8	3.34
2	32.0	2.83
3	24.0	4.53

What would you expect the mean number of quotations per page to be for the whole book, giving limits as determined by the standard error?

As there are 430 pages of quotations, deduce how many quotations you could expect in the volume and note how your result compares with the reference on the back cover to '12000 or so quotations in this dictionary'.

5.2 The cost (in pence) of a random sample of 11 popular paperbacks published in 1974 was:

$$30 \quad 25 \quad 35 \quad 35 \quad 75 \quad 35 \quad 30 \quad 40 \quad 35 \quad 40 \quad 60$$

On this basis, what are the 95% confidence limits for the mean cost of all such paperbacks that year?

Hence, assuming 10% inflation, what sum of money would you have set aside to be reasonably sure of being able to buy 500 paperbacks in 1975?

How large a sample should you have taken if the 95% confidence limits were to be not more than 10p apart?

5.3 The number of issues of junior books from a library on a random sample of 35 days were:

72	20	34	26	27	31	21
28	46	25	13	24	33	70
15	11	20	17	11	50	74
48	45	19	48	72	34	43
41	30	22	27	39	54	33

Determine the 95% confidence limits for the probable mean number of daily issues throughout the year.

A further five samples were taken, each including observations on 35 days, with the following results:

Sample	$\bar{X}$	s
1	35.60	9.92
2	44.00	21.82
3	35.13	16.19
4	43.33	17.62
5	35.13	12.62

From these five samples, calculate a maximum value for the mean number of issues of junior non-fiction books per day as determined by the standard error.

5.4 A random sample of short loans was examined and the number of times each item had been used was as follows:

$$2 \ 5 \ 1 \ 4 \ 2 \ 6 \ 6 \ 3 \ 2 \ 3 \ 9 \ 5$$

Determine the 95% confidence limits for the probable mean number of times a volume in the short-loan collection is used.

A further five samples were taken, each including 12 observations, with the following results:

Sample	$\bar{X}$	s
1	3.00	2.00
2	2.08	1.51
3	3.50	2.24
4	3.92	2.23
5	3.08	2.43

From these five samples, calculate a minimum value for the mean number of times a volume is used, as determined by the standard error.

5.5 The heights (in inches) of a random sample of 10 books were:

$$8 \ 8\tfrac{3}{4} \ 8\tfrac{1}{4} \ 7\tfrac{1}{2} \ 9 \ 9\tfrac{3}{4} \ 7\tfrac{1}{2} \ 8\tfrac{3}{4} \ 9\tfrac{1}{2} \ 10$$

What is the minimum height of shelf you would need in order to be sure of being able to accommodate 95% of the books in the collection?

Chapter 6

PROBABILITY

In the last chapter, inferences were made about a whole population on the basis of observations made on samples drawn from the population. The inferences could not be made with complete certainty but a fair degree of accuracy was achieved by basing the calculations on the 95% confidence limits.

Nevertheless, all that can be said from observations made on samples is that the population will *probably* have such-and-such properties. We are therefore concerned with *probability*.

When we sample a variable, the probability of the variable having a particular characteristic in that sample is defined as the number of observations of that characteristic compared with the total number of observations in the sample, ie

$$\text{Probability} = \frac{\text{Number of observations with characteristic}}{\text{Total number of observations}}$$

For example, the variable may be the number of books borrowed by various users when visiting the library. Suppose that each of ten library users is asked as he leaves the library how many books he has borrowed and that the answers are:

$$3 \quad 1 \quad 2 \quad 3 \quad 4 \quad 2 \quad 5 \quad 3 \quad 4 \quad 3$$

Or, to make it clearer by rearranging into an array:

$$1 \quad 2 \quad 2 \quad 3 \quad 3 \quad 3 \quad 3 \quad 4 \quad 4 \quad 5$$

In this particular sample of 10 users, if the characteristic of interest were a user borrowing three books, the probability of observing that characteristic is determined by the fact that four out of the ten users borrowed that number of volumes. Applying the above expression, the probability that any particular one of the ten should be carrying three books when questioned is given by:

68

Probability (of having 3 books) = $\frac{4}{10}$ (or 0.4 as a decimal)

Similarly, the probability that he would be found to be carrying four books is $\frac{2}{10}$ (or 0.2).

The probability that he would be carrying either four books or three books is governed by the *addition law of probability*. Readers who are familiar with Boolean algebra will recognize this situation as involving OR logic and requires summation. Since the probability of having four books is $\frac{2}{10}$ and the probability of having three books is $\frac{4}{10}$:

$$\text{Probability (of having either 4 or 3 books)} = \frac{2}{10} + \frac{4}{10}$$
$$= \frac{6}{10} \text{ (or 0.6)}$$

If two users (A and B) were stopped, the probability of the first one (A) having four books and the second one (B) having three books is governed by the *multiplication law of probability*. Again, readers familiar with Boolean algebra will recognize this situation as involving AND logic and requires multiplication. Since the probability of A having four books is $\frac{2}{10}$ and that of B having three books is $\frac{4}{10}$, then:

$$\text{Probability (of A having 4 and B having 3)} = \frac{2}{10} \times \frac{4}{10}$$
$$= \frac{8}{100} \text{ (or 0.08)}$$

Similarly:

$$\text{Probability (of A having 3 and B having 4)} = \frac{4}{10} \times \frac{2}{10}$$
$$= \frac{8}{100}$$

It is now possible to resolve the more complex situation of determining the probability, on stopping the two users A and B, that either A has four books and B has three books or, alternatively, that A has three books and B has four books. This involves the application of the multiplication law followed by application of the addition law. Thus:

Probability (of A having 4 and B having 3) $= \frac{2}{10} \times \frac{4}{10} = \frac{8}{100}$

Probability (of A having 3 and B having 4) $= \frac{4}{10} \times \frac{2}{10} = \frac{8}{100}$

Probability (of A having 3 or 4 and B having 4 or 3) $= \frac{8}{100} + \frac{8}{100} = \frac{16}{100}$

Thus, the probability of a characteristic occurring in a sample is based on counts of relevant observations and of total possible observations, followed, if necessary, by the application of one or both of the two laws of probability. Obviously, the characteristic of interest must be clearly defined at the outset. It should also be appreciated that the

69

probability so determined applies only to the sample on which the observations were made. The probability of observing the characteristic in another sample may well be different.

The above data can, of course, be represented graphically in the form of a histogram which approximates to a normal distribution (Figure 6.1).

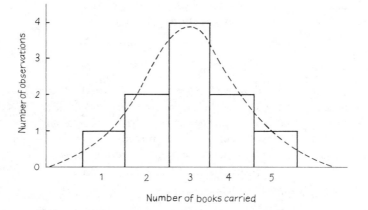

Figure 6.1: Distribution of book-borrowing data

If the characteristic that is sought is that the number of books carried is between two standard deviations less than the mean and two standard deviations more than the mean, we can make use of the known property of a normal distribution that approximately 95% of all observations lie within two standard deviations of the mean. Hence we can say that:

Probability (of observation falling between $\mu - 2\sigma$ and $\mu + 2\sigma$)

$$= \frac{\text{Number of observations with characteristic}}{\text{Total number of observations}}$$

$$= \frac{95}{100}$$

Measures of probability are therefore related to the 95% confidence limits. If we can measure probability and, from that, deduce the mean and standard deviation, we can find the value of the variable at the confidence limits.

Suppose that we are interested to find out how many library users

70

may be expected to borrow three books. The characteristic sought is the carrying of three books and it would be considered a 'success' if a user were found to have three books in his possession. Then, in the sample referred to above, the 'probability of success' (represented by the letter p) is given by:

$$p \text{ (probability of having 3 books)} = \tfrac{4}{10}$$

As previously noted, the probability of finding a characteristic will vary from one sample to another, but we shall take this value to be the mean of the distribution of probabilities of success.

The standard deviation of that distribution is known as the *standard error of the probability of success* and is represented by the expression:

$$\sqrt{\frac{p \cdot q}{n}}$$

in which n is the number of observations in the sample

$\qquad p$ is the probability of success

$\qquad q$ is the probability of failure

'Failure' in this example will mean that a user is carrying any number of books except 3. The probability of failure, q, may be found in one of two ways:

1   The probability of finding each value of the variable other than the sought one can be determined and the total probability of failure found by applying the addition law of probability. Hence:

$$q \text{ (probability of having 1 or 2 or 4 or 5 books)} = \tfrac{1}{10} + \tfrac{2}{10} + \tfrac{2}{10} + \tfrac{1}{10}$$

$$= \tfrac{6}{10}$$

2   The procedure of the last section could be lengthy if there were a large number of different values of the variable. This difficulty can be avoided if it is appreciated that the total probability is unity — as can be seen by summing the probabilities of all the varibles:

$$\tfrac{1}{10} + \tfrac{2}{10} + \tfrac{3}{10} + \tfrac{2}{10} + \tfrac{1}{10} = \tfrac{10}{10} = 1$$

The probability of failure can therefore be found by subtracting the probability of success from unity, ie

$$q = 1 - p$$

Hence, in the above example:

$$q = 1 - \tfrac{4}{10}$$
$$= \tfrac{6}{10}$$

The standard error of probability of success can now be found:

$$\text{Standard error} = \sqrt{\frac{\tfrac{4}{10} \times \tfrac{6}{10}}{10}}$$
$$= \sqrt{\tfrac{24}{1000}}$$
$$= 0.155$$

Now that the mean and the standard deviation for the distribution of the probability of success are known, the 95% confidence limits can be determined as:

$$\tfrac{4}{10} - 2 \times 0.155 \quad \text{and} \quad \tfrac{4}{10} + 2 \times 0.155$$

ie 0.09 and 0.71

The probability of a user having three books is, therefore, not likely to be less than 0.09, nor more than 0.71.

If it is remembered that:

$$\text{Probability} = \frac{\text{Number of observations of characteristic}}{\text{Total number of observations}}$$

the minimum number and maximum number of users in any population who may be expected to be carrying three books can be determined by rearranging that expression to the form:

Probability × Total number of observations
= Number of observations of characteristic

Hence, out of 1000 library users, the minimum number who could be expected (with 95% confidence) to borrow three books would be:

$$0.09 \times 1000 = 90$$

And the maximum number who could be expected (with 95% confidence) to borrow three books would be:

$$0.71 \times 1000 = 710$$

The fact that the limits to the estimated result in this example are extremely wide should be heeded as a warning that this type of calculation should be performed only if the population concerned is large. The sample taken can then be made as large as conveniently possible, the consequence of which is that the standard error is made smaller and the 95% confidence limits are made closer.

Suppose that, in the example, a sample of 500 users had been taken and the probability of success had been the same, the standard error would have been:

$$\sqrt{\frac{\frac{4}{10} \times \frac{6}{10}}{500}}$$

$$= 0.022$$

The 95% confidence limits would then have been:

$$\frac{4}{10} - 2 \times 0.022 \quad \text{and} \quad \frac{4}{10} + 2 \times .022$$

ie   0.356   and   0.444

And, out of 1000 users, no fewer than 356 nor more than 444 would be expected to have three books.

Large populations in which there may be some characteristic of interest can easily be envisaged, eg bibliographic records in computerized databases; document holdings of major libraries; annual issues; library membership etc.

The above theory was developed on the basis of a normal distribution. However, there are other special forms of distribution that may be met and which can be dealt with by probability theory.

Uniform distribution

Suppose that there are four books with identical covers on a shelf and that the books are identified as Book 1, Book 2, Book 3, and Book 4. If one book is to be selected, they all have an equal opportunity of being chosen and the probability of Book 1 being chosen will therefore be $\frac{1}{4}$. This is expressed as:

$$P(1) = \frac{1}{4}$$

Similarly:

$$P(2) = \frac{1}{4}$$
$$P(3) = \frac{1}{4}$$
and:
$$P(4) = \frac{1}{4}$$

In general terms, it could be stated that the book number is represented by x and the probability of Book x being selected is represented

73

by $P(x)$. Diagrammatically, the information can be plotted in the form of a *probability distribution* which is analogous to a frequency distribution. Figure 6.2 is a probability distribution showing the probabilities of each of the four books selected. Since the probabilities are equal, a *uniform distribution* is produced.

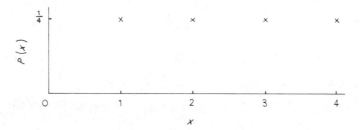

Figure 6.2: Uniform probability distribution

Note again that the total probability, ie the probability of all four books being selected, is unity:

$$P = P(1) + P(2) + P(3) + P(4)$$
$$= \tfrac{1}{4} + \tfrac{1}{4} + \tfrac{1}{4} + \tfrac{1}{4}$$
$$= 1$$

Binomial distribution

Suppose that a library user selects books by taking them at random from the shelves and reading the blurb to decide whether or not to take a book from the library.

Suppose that, from a large number of observations, the probability of taking a book after reading the blurb has been found to be $\tfrac{1}{3}$. The probability of leaving it is therefore $\tfrac{2}{3}$.

Suppose that the reader looks at only four books. The problem is to determine the probability of the reader taking 1, 2, 3, or 4 books from the library.

Let T be used to indicate that a book is taken and L be used to indicate that a book is left behind.

The probability of not taking the first book is $\tfrac{2}{3}$ — as also are the probabilities of not taking the second, third and fourth books. The total probability of not taking any of the four will be found by applying the multiplication law, ie the probability of taking no book — $P(0)$

– is the probability of Book 1 not being taken AND Book 2 not being taken AND Book 3 not being taken AND Book 4 not being taken. Then:

$$P(0) = P(L) \times P(L) \times P(L) \times P(L)$$
$$= \tfrac{2}{3} \times \tfrac{2}{3} \times \tfrac{2}{3} \times \tfrac{2}{3}$$
$$= \tfrac{16}{81}$$

If only one book is taken, it may be the first – in which case the probability of taking it and no other is $P(T) \times P(L) \times P(L) \times P(L)$.

On the other hand, if it were the second book that was taken, the probability of taking it and no other is $P(L) \times P(T) \times P(L) \times P(L)$.

After similarly considering the taking of only the third or only the fourth book, the total probability of taking only one of the four – $P(1)$ – will be found by applying the addition law.

Then:

$$P(1) = P(T) \times P(L) \times P(L) \times P(L)$$
$$+ P(L) \times P(T) \times P(L) \times P(L)$$
$$+ P(L) \times P(L) \times P(T) \times P(L)$$
$$+ P(L) \times P(L) \times P(L) \times P(T)$$

Substituting the numerical values given above:

$$P(1) = (\tfrac{1}{3} \times \tfrac{2}{3} \times \tfrac{2}{3} \times \tfrac{2}{3}) + (\tfrac{2}{3} \times \tfrac{1}{3} \times \tfrac{2}{3} \times \tfrac{2}{3}) + (\tfrac{2}{3} \times \tfrac{2}{3} \times \tfrac{1}{3} \times \tfrac{2}{3})$$
$$+ (\tfrac{2}{3} \times \tfrac{2}{3} \times \tfrac{2}{3} \times \tfrac{1}{3})$$
$$= \tfrac{1}{3} \times (\tfrac{2}{3})^3 \times 4$$
$$= \tfrac{32}{81}$$

If any two books are taken, similar arguments will show that the total probability of taking two (and leaving two) books is given by:

$$P(2) = P(T) \times P(T) \times P(L) \times P(L)$$
$$+ P(T) \times P(L) \times P(T) \times P(L)$$
$$+ P(T) \times P(L) \times P(L) \times P(T)$$
$$+ P(L) \times P(T) \times P(T) \times P(L)$$
$$+ P(L) \times P(T) \times P(L) \times P(T)$$
$$+ P(L) \times P(L) \times P(T) \times P(T)$$

$$= (\tfrac{1}{3})^2 \times (\tfrac{2}{3})^2 \times 6$$

$$= \tfrac{24}{81}$$

The total probability of taking any three books and leaving the fourth is given by:

$$P(3) = P(T) \times P(T) \times P(T) \times P(L)$$
$$+ P(T) \times P(T) \times P(L) \times P(T)$$
$$+ P(T) \times P(L) \times P(T) \times P(T)$$
$$+ P(L) \times P(T) \times P(T) \times P(T)$$
$$= (\tfrac{1}{3})^3 \times \tfrac{2}{3} \times 4$$
$$= \tfrac{8}{81}$$

Finally, the total probability of taking all four books is given by:

$$P(4) = P(T) \times P(T) \times P(T) \times P(T)$$
$$= (\tfrac{1}{3})^4$$
$$= \tfrac{1}{81}$$

These results are shown diagrammatically in the probability distribution of Figure 6.3. This is a *binomial distribution*.

From this detailed knowledge of the probability distribution, it is possible to deduce information that is likely to be required. For example, if the interest were in a person taking at least one book, the person may take only one − or two, or three, or four. It was shown above that:

the probability of taking one book, ie $P(1)$ $= \tfrac{32}{81}$

the probability of taking two books, ie $P(2)$ $= \tfrac{24}{81}$

the probability of taking three books, ie $P(3)$ $= \tfrac{8}{81}$

the probability of taking four books, ie $P(4)$ $= \tfrac{1}{81}$

Hence, by applying the addition law, the probability of taking at least one book will be found as:

$$P(1) + P(2) + P(3) + P(4) = \tfrac{65}{81}$$

Now, remembering that:

$$\text{Probability} = \frac{\text{Number of observations with characteristic}}{\text{Total number of observations}}$$

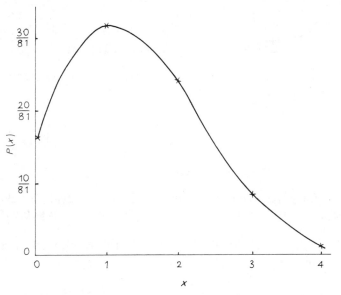

Figure 6.3: Distribution of probability of a person taking a specified number of books (x) from a library

and specifying that an 'observation' is a visit to the library and the 'characteristic' is the taking of one or more books, it will now be clear that:

$$\frac{\text{Number of observations with characteristic}}{\text{Total number of observations}} = \frac{65}{81}$$

Then, if the total number of observations were 81, the number of observations with the characteristic would be 65. In other words, out of 81 visits to the library, a person would take out one or more books on 65 occasions.

The same conclusion could have been reached more easily if it is remembered that the total probability is always unity. That is, in this example:

$$P(0) + P(1) + P(2) + P(3) + P(4) = 1$$

This is written more concisely as $\sum_{0}^{4} P(x)$ — meaning 'add together the probabilities for each of the values of the variable x from $x = 0$ up to and including $x = 4$'.

77

So:

$$\sum_0^4 P(x) = P(0) + P(1) + P(2) + P(3) + P(4)$$

Therefore, by taking $P(0)$ from each side of the equation, we find that the probability that we are seeking is:

$$P(1) + P(2) + P(3) + P(4)$$

$$= \sum_0^4 P(x) - P(0)$$

$$= 1 - P(0)$$

But, as $P(0)$ was found to be equal to $\frac{16}{81}$, the probability of taking at least one book will therefore be $(1 - \frac{16}{81})$ — or $\frac{65}{81}$ as was found previously.

Similarly, the probability of taking less than three books can be found either as:

$$P(0) + P(1) + P(2)$$

or as:

$$\sum_0^4 P(x) - [P(3) + P(4)]$$

ie
$$1 - [P(3) + P(4)]$$

A general expression for determining the probability of observing a variable of value x is:

$$P(x) = \frac{n!}{x!.(n-x)!} \cdot p^x \cdot q^{n-x}$$

where

x	is any value of a variable
$P(x)$	is the probability of observing the variable of value x
n	is the number of observations
p	is the probability of success
q	is the probability of failure
$n!$	is $n(n-1)(n-2)\dots 1$
$0!$	$= 1$
p^0	$= 1$
p^1	$= p$

78

For example, taking $n = 4, p = \frac{1}{3}, q = \frac{2}{3}$ as before, the probability of taking exactly three books from the library will be given by:

$$P(3) = \frac{4 \times 3 \times 2 \times 1}{(3 \times 2 \times 1) \times 1} \times (\tfrac{1}{3})^3 \times (\tfrac{2}{3})^{4-3}$$

$$= 4 \times (\tfrac{1}{3})^3 \times (\tfrac{2}{3})^1$$

$$= 4 \times \tfrac{1}{27} \times \tfrac{2}{3}$$

$$= \tfrac{8}{81}$$

Just as the normal distribution was seen to have a mean that locates it on the horizontal axis and a standard deviation that defines its dispersion, so the binomial distribution has a mean and standard deviation. The mean for the binomial distribution is equal to np and the standard deviation is equal to $\sqrt{npq}$. Therefore, in the above example, where:

$$n = 4$$
$$p = \tfrac{1}{3}$$
$$q = \tfrac{2}{3}$$

the mean number of books taken from the library would be given by:

$$\mu = np$$
$$= 4 \times \tfrac{1}{3}$$
$$= 1.33$$

and the standard deviation of the number of books taken from the library would be given by:

$$\sigma = \sqrt{4 \times \tfrac{1}{3} \times \tfrac{2}{3}}$$
$$= 0.943$$

Example One reader in 32 asks the librarian for help. Sixteen readers use the library each hour. What is the mean number of enquiries per hour? If each enquiry takes 30 minutes to deal with, could the librarian be 95% sure of managing single-handed? What is the probability of no one asking for help in any given hour?

A 'success' will be a reader asking for help. The probability of success is therefore 1/32.

The number of observations per hour = 16
The mean number of enquiries per hour will therefore be:

$$\mu = np$$
$$= 16 \times \tfrac{1}{32}$$
$$= \tfrac{1}{2}$$

The standard deviation of the number of enquiries per hour will be:

$$\sigma = \sqrt{npq}$$
$$= \sqrt{16 \times \tfrac{1}{32} \times \tfrac{31}{32}}$$
$$= \sqrt{0.4844}$$
$$= 0.696$$

The maximum number of enquiries that may be expected in any one hour with 95% confidence is:

$$\mu + 2\sigma = 0.5 + 2 \times 0.696$$
$$= 0.5 + 1.392$$
$$= 1.892$$

But since it takes 30 minutes to deal with each enquiry, the time taken to handle 1.892 enquiries is 56.76 minutes.

Even in these extreme circumstances, the librarian should be able to manage and he would not be under such pressure very frequently since the probability of there being two requests in an hour is $P(2)$, which is only:

$$\frac{16!}{2!\,14!} \left(\frac{1}{32}\right)^{2} \left(\frac{31}{32}\right)^{14} = 0.088$$

Such heavy demand will occur therefore only once in every $\dfrac{1}{0.088}$ hours, ie less than once in every eleven hours. On the other hand, the probability of no one asking for help in any particular hour is:

$$P(0) = \frac{16!}{0!\,16!} \left(\frac{1}{32}\right)^{0} \left(\frac{31}{32}\right)^{16}$$
$$= 1 \times 1 \times \left(\tfrac{31}{32}\right)^{16}$$
$$= 0.6$$

Therefore, if the librarian worked ten hours a day, he would expect to have no enquiries in six of those hours, be under quite heavy pressure answering enquiries for about one hour and, on average, spend about one quarter of his time dealing with enquiries.

80

Poisson distribution

A special situation arises if the number of observations (n) is very large and the probability of success (p) is very small. Under these circumstances the binomial distribution tends towards another distribution — the *Poisson distribution*. In the Poisson distribution, the probability of observing the variable of value x is given by:

$$P(x) = e^{-\mu} \cdot \frac{\mu^x}{x!}$$

where e is the exponential constant ($= 2.718$).

So:

$$\Sigma P(x) = P(0) + P(1) + P(2) + P(4) \ldots$$

$$= e^{-\mu} \cdot \frac{\mu^0}{0!} + e^{-\mu} \cdot \frac{\mu^1}{1!} + e^{-\mu} \cdot \frac{\mu^2}{2!} + e^{-\mu} \cdot \frac{\mu^3}{3!} \ldots$$

$$= e^{-\mu}(1 + \mu + \frac{\mu^2}{2} + \frac{\mu^3}{6} + \frac{\mu^4}{24} \ldots)$$

This expression is applicable if the number of observations (n) is greater than 40 and the probability of success (p) is less than 0.1, but the larger the value of n, the more accurate will be the result.

The mean for the Poisson distribution is given by the same formula as for the binomial distribution, ie

$$\mu = np$$

However, because of the special conditions in a Poisson distribution, its standard deviation can be stated in a different way. For the binomial distribution:

$$\sigma = \sqrt{npq}$$

But, in the Poisson distribution, p is less than 0.1 and therefore q is greater than 0.9 and approaches 1. Hence, if we put $q = 1$,

$$\sigma = \sqrt{np}$$

and since $np = \mu$, we find that

$$\sigma = \sqrt{\mu}$$

Example If the average demand for copies of reprints of articles is 9, what is the probability of there being no requests for reprints of an article? How many copies should be ordered from the publisher so as

81

to be 95% sure of meeting the demand (assuming a Poisson distribution)?

Mean demand for copies of articles = $\mu = 9$

Probability of an article not being required = $P(0) = e^{-9} \cdot \dfrac{9^0}{0!}$

$$= 0.0001$$

(Note that the value of $e^{-\mu}$ is found from the table in Appendix 8.)

Standard deviation of demand for copies = $\sigma = \sqrt{\mu}$

$$= \sqrt{9}$$

$$= 3$$

Therefore, the upper 95% confidence limit $= \mu + 2\sigma$

$$= 9 + 6$$

$$= 15$$

Hence, 15 copies of the article should be ordered in order to satisfy the expected demand.

Examples

6.1   In a random sample of 10 shelves, the numbers of books per shelf were:

               27 24 25 28 24 23 29 26 26 26

  (a) What is the probability of a shelf having exactly 24 books?

  (b) What is the probability of a shelf having less than 24 books?

  (c) What is the probability of a shelf having either 24 or 25 books?

6.2   The number of books on each of a number of shelves in a library is given by:

No of books per shelf	19	20	21	22	23	24	25	26	27	28	29	30
No of shelves	2	3	7	5	14	11	12	9	6	6	3	2

  (a) What is the probability of a shelf having exactly 24 books?

  (b) What is the probability of a shelf having less than 24 books?

  (c) What is the probability of a shelf having either 24 or 25 books?

6.3   A bibliography contains 2055 references. Out of a random sample of 95 of these references, 11 were found to be in a foreign language. What is the maximum number of foreign language items that you might, with 95% confidence, expect to find in the whole bibliography?

6.4 The *International who's who* 1970-71 contains about 15,000 names. Out of a random sample of 81 names, 18 were British. What are the minimum and maximum number of British people for whom you might, with 95% confidence, expect to find an entry?

6.5 There are 20,000 books in a library. Out of a random sample of 500 books, 20 were found to be in need of repair. What is the maximum number of books from the whole library that you might, with 95% confidence, expect to be in need of repair?

6.6 Out of a random sample of 500 people entering a library, 75 were juniors. What is (a) the maximum number of junior readers (b) the maximum number of adult readers that you would, with 95% confidence, expect to find in a total reading population of 18,000?

6.7 Out of 2000 sheets of paper that passed through a duplicating machine, a random sample of 100 sheets were checked and 5 were found to be blank. What is the minimum number of the 2000 sheets that you could, with 95% confidence, expect to be properly printed? How many sheets would you expect to have to pass through the machine in order to be reasonably sure of obtaining 2000 properly printed sheets?

6.8 When a pilot survey of library users was carried out by asking a random sample of 150 to complete and return a questionnaire, 97 replies were received. What is the maximum number of replies that you might, with 95% confidence, expect to receive if all 4568 of the registered users of the library were surveyed? What size of sample would you need to take to ensure that you had at least 1000 returns?

6.9 On each visit to the library, a reader looks at 3 books and the probability of borrowing a book is $\frac{1}{4}$. On how many occasions out of 128 visits does he borrow (a) 2 books or more (b) less than 3 books?

6.10 On average, only 1 carrel out of three available in a library is free at any time. What is the probability that (a) a reader will have to wait for a free carrel (b) there is more than one carrel free?

6.11 If 5% of books returned to a library are overdue, what is the probability that a reader returning 4 books will have at least one overdue?

6.12 A public library finds that only 1 in a 1000 of visitors to the library asks for help from the staff. If there are 500 readers per day, what is the probability of there being two or more who seek help?

6.13 A typist makes, on average, 2 mistakes per page. On how many pages of a 50 page report would you expect to find errors?

6.14 Of 200 books on set text, 9 were not used. Assuming a Poisson distribution, what was the mean number of times a text was used? How many were likely to be used more than once?

6.15 Readers enter a library at an average rate of 120 per hour. How many can be expected to enter in one minute? What is the probability that this number actually enter in a given one minute period?

6.16 If a reader selected 200 reports at random and found that only 3 related to his sphere of interest, what sum would you have to allocate to purchase all reports likely to be of interest in a year in which 5200 reports are expected to be published at a cost of 50p each? If the reports arrive in equal weekly batches, how often will there be more than one item of interest?

6.17 If, in pursuing literature searches, it is found that only one in three of the items found normally prove to be of interest, what are the chances of there being less than three useful items in a list of 20?

Chapter 7

STATISTICAL TESTING

It is often necessary to compare two sets of data to determine whether they are comparable or whether a significant difference exists. For example, we may wish to know whether or not the mean salary of librarians in Newcastle differs significantly from the mean salary of librarians in the country as a whole or from the mean salary of librarians in London. Or we may wish to know whether, in a school, the number of books borrowed from the library by sixth formers differs significantly from the mean number of books borrowed by all pupils. Or we may wish to know whether a search of a computer database costs significantly more between (say) 2 pm and 4 pm, (ie busy times for the computer) than at other times of the day.

Solution of such problems is by means of a statistical test, the first step of which is to formulate a *null hypothesis* and its *alternative*. The null hypothesis is an assumption that there is no real difference between the two sets of data concerned whilst the alternative is that there is a significant difference that cannot reasonably be accounted for by chance. It is the purpose of a statistical test to decide whether to accept or to reject the null hypothesis.

A difference may well be found to exist between two quantities, but the question is whether or not that difference is significant. If a person A had a salary of £6000 per annum and a person B had a salary of £6050 per annum, the reaction of an observer would be that the salaries are not significantly different. However, if A's salary were £6000 and B's salary were £10,000, the observer's reaction would be that the two salaries are significantly different. Somewhere between £6050 and £10,000, the interpretation of the difference changes — the question is, where?

Since 95% of observations in a distribution lie between two standard deviations below the mean and two standard deviations above the mean, we would not attach any significance to an observation we made that fell within that range. For example, if the mean cost of books were £10 and the standard deviation were £3, we would expect the majority of book purchases to lie between £4 and £16. An account for (say) £12, though different from the mean, would not strike us as being significant and would be paid without query. On the other hand, an account for £20 under those circumstances would be considered significant and investigated to determine whether it was merely one of the $2\frac{1}{2}\%$ of observations that fall by chance beyond two standard deviations above the mean or whether the volume had some special feature that made it unusually expensive.

The points that lie two standard deviations on either side of the mean can therefore be taken as thresholds of significance (A and B in Figure 7.1). Any observation between those points is not significant whilst any observation outside those points may be deemed to be significant.

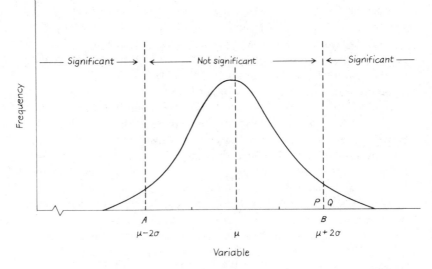

Figure 7.1: Frequency distribution showing 0.05 significance level

Since 95% of observations are not significant, 5% are significant. Expressed as a decimal, 5% is 0.05 and the two points are known as the 5% or 0.05 *significance level.*

However, it seems hardly justifiable to draw a hard and fast line and say that, whilst the value of the variable at P is not significant, the value

86

of the variable at Q is significant. Or, being more specific, could we reasonably say that a book costing £15.99 is not significant, whereas a book costing £16.01 is significant?

To resolve that difficulty, a second significance level is commonly referred to — the 1% or 0.01 *significance level*. This marks the points between which lie 99% of all observations (Figure 7.2).

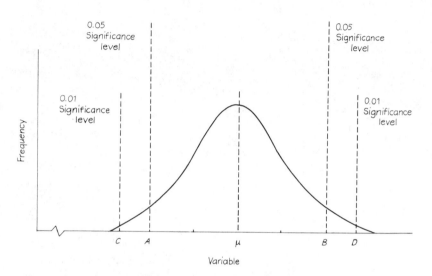

Figure 7.2: Frequency distribution showing 0.05 and 0.01 significance levels

As before, any observation between A and B is not significant. An observation between A and C or between B and D is said to be 'significant at the 0.05 level' whilst an observation beyond C or beyond D is said to be 'significant at the 0.01 level'. More importance must be attached to significance at the 0.01 level than to significance only at the 0.05 level.

Reverting now to statistical testing, the next step is to calculate a statistic from the data concerned. That calculated value is then compared with a sampling distribution of that statistic, the values of the significance levels for which are given in statistical tables (eg Lindley and Miller). If the calculated value lies between the 0.05 significance levels, the null hypothesis is accepted and if it lies outside the

87

0.01 significance levels, the null hypothesis is rejected. However, if the calculated value of the statistic lies between the 0.05 and the 0.01 significance levels, we are in a state of uncertainty. There is insufficient indication that the null hypothesis should be rejected, yet neither can it justifiably be accepted. If such a situation arises and it is possible to collect more data, it would be desirable to do so and hope that a re-calculation on the basis of a larger collection of data will provide a more decisive result (Figure 7.3).

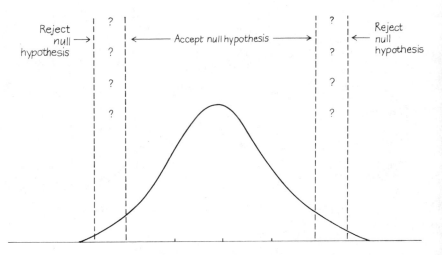

Figure 7.3: Sampling distribution of statistic showing decisions regarding null hypothesis

One-tailed and two-tailed tests
In looking at statistical tables, reference will be found to *one-tail* and *two-tails* and the values of the 0.05 and 0.01 significance levels will be seen to be different according to whether two tails of the distribution or only one tail is involved.

A two-tailed test would be exemplified by an investigation of the number of documents in a collection having *either* many fewer *or* many more keywords than average to describe their subject content. As both possibilities are of interest, the 5% of observations that are significant are equally distributed between the two tails of the distribution, $2\frac{1}{2}\%$ being in each of the shaded areas of Figure 7.4.

In some cases, only one end of the distribution may be of interest, as
88

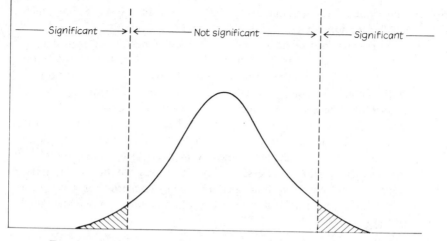

*Figure 7.4: Distribution showing the 0.05 significance levels in
a two-tailed test*

for example when only the number of documents described by many
more keywords than average is being investigated. This would be a
one-tailed test and, since only one possibility is of interest, the 5%
of observations that are significant are contained in the one tail shaded
in Figure 7.5.

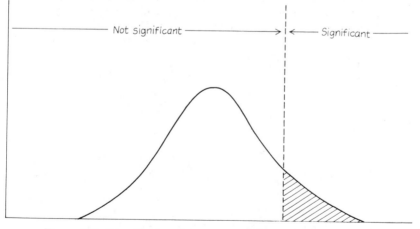

*Figure 7.5: Distribution showing the 0.05 significance level in
a one-tailed test*

The value of the variable at the 0.05 significance level is thus much smaller for a one-tailed test than for a two-tailed test.

For a given set of data, various tests may be performed according to the point of view being investigated. For example, the average ratio of library staff to number of readers for the several libraries in an organization could be compared with the recommended norm in order to determine whether they appeared to be *either* understaffed *or* overstaffed. That would be a two-tailed test. The library staff could use the same data to decide whether they were understaffed (and overworked) – without being concerned if they were overstaffed. Conversely, the management could use the same data to decide whether the libraries were overstaffed – without perhaps being concerned if they were understaffed. In either case, the investigation would involve a one-tailed test.

Standard normal distribution
Since the significance and standard deviation are related, it is often helpful in determining significance to use a simplified arrangement of the normal distribution, known as the *standard normal distribution*. In the standard normal distribution, the mean is always zero, the standard deviation is always unity, and the range is therefore approximately six (ie six times the standard deviation). It is shown in Figure 7.6.

Any normal distribution can be converted to a standard normal distribution by converting the X values of the normal distribution into Z values for plotting the standard normal distribution by the equation:

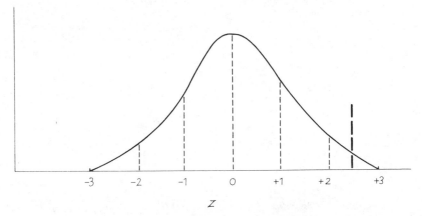

Figure 7.6: Standard normal distribution

$$Z = \frac{\text{Variable} - \text{Mean}}{\text{Standard deviation}}$$

For the distribution of a population:

$$Z = \frac{x - \mu}{\sigma}$$

For the distribution of a sample:

$$Z = \frac{X - \bar{X}}{s}$$

For the sampling distribution of the mean:

$$Z = \frac{\bar{X} - \mu}{\sigma_{\bar{X}}}$$

Hence the distribution of Figure 7.7 with a mean of 50 and a standard deviation of 6 would become the standard normal distribution as in Figure 7.6.

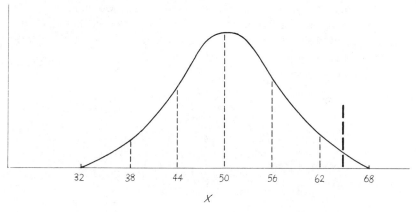

Figure 7.7: Example of a normal distribution

A value of X of 65, as shown in Figure 7.7, would appear in the standard normal distribution, as shown in Figure 7.6, at:

$$Z = \frac{65 - 50}{6}$$

$$= 2\tfrac{1}{2}$$

91

A value of X of 42 would appear in the standard normal distribution at:

$$Z = \frac{42 - 50}{6}$$

$$= -1\tfrac{1}{3}$$

Z-Tests

A Z-Test is used to determine whether or not the mean of a sample is significantly different from the mean of the population from which it is taken. It is applicable only for large samples in which the number of observations is 30 or more.

The precise form of calculation will depend on the particular problem that is being investigated as the following examples will show.

1 **Example** In *Economics abstracts*, July 1972, the mean length of abstract is 79.56 words with a standard deviation of 24.80. A random sample of thirty of the abstracts in German language has a mean length of 67.47 words. It is required to test whether there is any significant difference between the random sample of abstracts in German and the whole population of abstracts in English, French and German.

The null hypothesis is that there is no difference other than that due to chance between the length of German language abstracts and the length of all abstracts.

The data provided are:

$$\mu = 79.56$$
$$\sigma = 24.80$$
$$\bar{X} = 67.47$$
$$n = 30$$

A value of Z is calculated using the expression:

$$Z = \frac{\bar{X} - \mu}{\sigma/\sqrt{n}}$$

Hence:

$$Z = \frac{67.47 - 79.56}{24.80/\sqrt{30}}$$

$$= -2.67$$

This is a two-tailed test since the average German abstract may be either longer or shorter than the average abstract in the whole population. From the last line of the t-distribution (Appendix 5), it will be seen that the 0.05 value and the 0.01 value of Z for a two-tailed test are 2.000 and 2.600 respectively. These values apply to the upper end of the distribution where Z is positive but, if $\bar{X}$ is less than μ, Z will be negative. At the lower end of the distribution therefore, the 0.05 and 0.01 significance levels of Z are -2.000 and -2.600 respectively.

Since the calculated value of Z lies outside the 0.01 significance level (Figure 7.8), it may be concluded that the null hypothesis is to be rejected and the alternative hypothesis is to be accepted. The length of the German language abstracts is significantly less than for the whole population of abstracts.

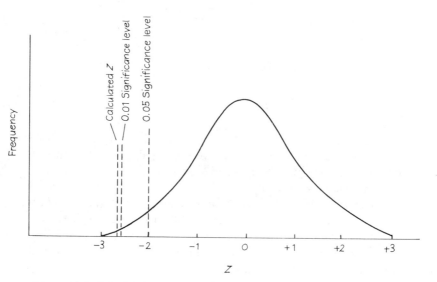

Figure 7.8: Standard normal distribution showing significance levels and value of Z calculated from raw data

2 **Example** In *Economics abstracts*, July 1972, the mean length of abstract is 79.56 words. A random sample of thirty of the abstracts in German language has a mean length of 67.47 words and a standard

deviation of 22.4. It is required to test whether there is any significant difference between the length of German language abstracts and the abstracts in general.

The null hypothesis is that there is no difference other than that due to chance.

The data provided are:

$$\mu = 79.56$$
$$\bar{X} = 67.47$$
$$s = 22.4$$
$$n = 30$$

Since the standard deviation of the population is not known, the standard deviation for the sample may be used as a rough estimate in order to determine Z from the expression:

$$Z = \frac{\bar{X} - \mu}{s/\sqrt{n}}$$

Hence:

$$Z = \frac{67.47 - 79.56}{22.4/\sqrt{30}}$$

$$= -2.95$$

The calculated value of Z can then be compared with the Z values for the 0.05 and 0.01 significance levels and, as in the previous example, the null hypothesis must be rejected.

3 Instead of comparing the mean of a sample with the mean of the population from which it has been taken, a comparison may be required between the means of two samples. For example, the mean time taken to classify a document by a sample of persons familiar with the classification scheme used may be compared with the mean time to classify a document by a sample of persons who have not used that particular classification scheme before.

In this case, the expression for Z is rather more complex:

$$Z = \frac{\bar{X}_1 - \bar{X}_2}{\sigma_D}$$

In this expression, it will be clear that $\bar{X}_1$ and $\bar{X}_2$ are the means of the two samples but the meaning of σ_D needs some explanation.

If a large number of pairs of samples were taken, the differences between the means of those pairs would form a frequency distribution — the sampling distribution of the differences between two means. The standard error of that sampling distribution is conveniently written as σ_D.

The standard error of the sampling distribution of the differences is related to the standard errors for the two samples by the expression:

$$\sigma_D{}^2 = \sigma_{\bar{X}_1}{}^2 + \sigma_{\bar{X}_2}{}^2$$

$$= \frac{\sigma_1{}^2}{n_1} + \frac{\sigma_2{}^2}{n_2}$$

where n_1 and n_2 are the numbers of observations in the two samples taken respectively from two populations with standard deviations σ_1 and σ_2.

So:

$$\sigma_D = \sqrt{\frac{\sigma_1{}^2}{n_1} + \frac{\sigma_2{}^2}{n_2}}$$

Or, if the two samples are taken from the same population:

$$\sigma_D = \sigma\sqrt{\frac{1}{n_1} + \frac{1}{n_2}}$$

Hence:

$$Z = \frac{\bar{X}_1 - \bar{X}_2}{\sigma\sqrt{\dfrac{1}{n_1} + \dfrac{1}{n_2}}}$$

If σ is not known, the standard deviations of the samples can be used instead but that is strictly applicable only for samples of at least 30 observations. In that case, the standard error of the sampling distribution of the differences is given by:

$$s_D{}^2 = s_{\bar{X}_1}{}^2 + s_{\bar{X}_2}{}^2$$

$$= \frac{s_1{}^2}{n_1} + \frac{s_2{}^2}{n_2}$$

Hence:

$$Z = \frac{\bar{X}_1 - \bar{X}_2}{\sqrt{\dfrac{s_1^2}{n_1} + \dfrac{s_2^2}{n_2}}}$$

Example It is required to know whether abstracts in *Economics abstracts* which are written in German are significantly different in length from those written in English. A random sample of 30 abstracts written in German had a mean length of 72.5 words and standard deviation of 26.85, whilst a random sample of 30 abstracts written in English had a mean length of 80.5 words and a standard deviation of 25.00.

The null hypothesis is that there is no difference between the two samples except that due to chance.

The data provided are:

$$\bar{X}_1 = 72.5$$
$$\bar{X}_2 = 80.5$$
$$s_1 = 26.85$$
$$s_2 = 25.00$$
$$n_1 = 30$$
$$n_2 = 30$$

Hence:

$$Z = \frac{72.5 - 80.5}{\sqrt{\dfrac{26.85^2}{30} + \dfrac{25.00^2}{30}}}$$

$$= -\frac{8}{\sqrt{44.86}}$$

$$= -1.2$$

Since the calculated value of Z does not exceed the 0.05 significance level of -2.000, the null hypothesis must be accepted. Consequently, the abstracts in German are not significantly shorter than the abstracts in English.

t-Tests

It was earlier pointed out that Z-tests are applicable only if there are thirty or more observations in the sample. As the number of observations decreases, the distribution of $\dfrac{\overline{X} - \mu}{\sigma/\sqrt{n}}$ diverges from a normal distribution.

It is known as *'Student's' distribution* or the *'t' distribution* and is represented by:

$$t = \frac{\overline{X} - \mu}{s/\sqrt{n}}$$

The precise form of the distribution depends on the number of *degrees of freedom* for the sample under investigation. The number of degrees of freedom for a sample is one less than the size of the sample, ie $n - 1$.

Hence, when a t value for a sample has been calculated, it is compared with the tabulated t values (Appendix 5) for the 0.05 and 0.01 significance on the line of the table for the appropriate number of degrees of freedom. It can then be determined whether or not the calculated value of t is significant at one or other of the levels.

Example It is required to know if the abstracts which are written in German in *Economics abstracts*, July 1972, are different in length from the average length of all abstracts. The mean length of all abstracts is 79.56 words. A random sample of 10 German abstracts has a mean length of 69.3 words and a standard deviation of 21.0.

The null hypothesis is that there is no difference between the length of German abstracts and the average length of all the abstracts.

The data provided are:

$$\mu = 79.56$$
$$\overline{X} = 69.3$$
$$s = 21.0$$
$$n = 10$$

Hence:

$$t = \frac{69.3 - 79.56}{21/\sqrt{10}}$$

$$= -1.56$$

The number of degrees of freedom in this case is 9 and it is a two-tailed test since the German abstracts could be either longer or shorter than the average abstract irrespective of language. From the table of t for 9 degrees of freedom and a two-tailed test, the 0.05 and 0.01 significance levels are 2.262 and 3.250 respectively. Since the calculated value

97

of t is -1.56, it would appear that the null hypothesis should be accepted. However, tests on small samples are less reliable than tests on large samples and, despite the above finding, a real difference may exist but there was insufficient evidence to prove it. Under such circumstances, a further test should be carried out, if possible using a larger sample.

When the random sample was increased in size to 20 observations, the mean length of German abstracts was found to be 68.8 and the standard deviation was 19.8.

The data are now:

$$\mu = 79.56$$
$$\bar{X} = 68.8$$
$$s = 19.8$$
$$n = 20$$

Hence: $$t = -2.43$$

From the table of t for 19 degrees of freedom, the 0.05 and 0.01 significance levels are 2.093 and 2.861 respectively. Thus, with a larger sample, some doubt is cast on the null hypothesis and there may well be a significant difference between the German abstracts and the population of abstracts of which they form a part.

Comparisons between pairs of small samples can be made by making use of the t distribution. For large samples, the equation used above was:

$$Z = \frac{\bar{X}_1 - \bar{X}_2}{\sqrt{\frac{s_1^2}{n_1} + \frac{s_2^2}{n_2}}}$$

For small samples, the equation takes a slightly different form, viz:

$$t = \frac{\bar{X}_1 - \bar{X}_2}{s \sqrt{\frac{1}{n_1} + \frac{1}{n_2}}}$$

where

$$s^2 = \frac{\Sigma(X_1 - \bar{X}_1)^2 + \Sigma(X_2 - \bar{X}_2)^2}{n_1 + n_2 - 2}$$

Using these equations and the observed data, t is calculated and the calculated value is compared with the table of t to determine its significance.

Example It is required to know whether abstracts in *Economics abstracts* which are written in German are significantly different in length from those written in English. The number of words in a random sample of 12 English abstracts and a random sample of 10 German abstracts are given in Figure 7.9 together with data derived therefrom. From the observations on the number of words it can be found that:

$$\overline{X}_1 = 87.6$$
$$\overline{X}_2 = 80.2$$

The null hypothesis is, of course, that there is no difference, other than that due to chance, between the two samples.

From the data in Figure 7.9, the value of the standard deviation can be calculated:

$$s^2 = \frac{8663.4 + 6250}{20}$$

$$= 745.67$$

Therefore:

$$s = 27.3$$

English Abstracts			German Abstracts		
X_1	$X_1 - \overline{X}_1$	$(X_1 - \overline{X}_1)^2$	X_2	$X_2 - \overline{X}_2$	$(X_2 - \overline{X}_2)^2$
65	−22.6	510.8	61	−19.2	368.6
93	5.4	29.2	97	16.8	282.2
147	59.4	3528.0	94	13.8	190.4
81	−6.6	43.6	90	9.8	96.0
71	−16.6	275.6	60	−20.2	408.0
107	19.4	376.4	113	32.8	1076.0
93	5.4	29.2	81	0.8	0.6
65	−22.6	510.8	113	32.8	1076.0
74	−13.6	185.0	62	−18.4	331.2
112	24.4	595.4	31	−49.2	2421.0
41	−46.6	2172.0			
102	14.4	207.4			
$\Sigma(X_1 - \overline{X}_1)^2 = 8663.4$			$\Sigma(X_2 - \overline{X}_2)^2 = 6250.0$		

Figure 7.9: Lengths of English and German abstracts from
Economics abstracts, *July 1972, and derived data*

Hence:

$$t = \frac{87.6 - 80.2}{27.3\sqrt{\frac{1}{12} + \frac{1}{10}}}$$

$$= 0.63$$

From the table of t for 20 (ie $10 - 1 + 12 - 1$) degrees of freedom and a two-tailed test, the 0.05 and 0.01 significance levels are 2.086 and 2.845 respectively. The calculated value of t is less than either of these values and therefore there appears to be no significant difference in length between the English and German abstracts.

F-Tests

Situations may arise in which the variances of two populations may need to be compared. Consider a distribution representing the number of hours per week spent by students in the library and the possible effect on that distribution resulting from the provision of reading lists. Some students may be stimulated by the help and spend more time in the library — others may be deterred by the length of the lists and spend less time in the library. If that were the case, the provision of reading lists would result in an increased dispersion of the observed data.

To investigate such a problem, two groups of students would be selected at random and one group would be provided with reading lists whilst the other group would not. A null hypothesis could then be formulated stating that there is no significant difference between the variances for the two groups. Such a hypothesis is tested by means of an *F-test*.

It will be recalled that the variance of a sample is given by:

$$s^2 = \frac{\Sigma(X - \bar{X})^2}{n - 1}$$

The ratio of the variances for two samples — Sample 1 and Sample 2 — is therefore given by:

$$\frac{s_1^2}{s_2^2} = \frac{\Sigma(X_1 - \bar{X}_1)^2}{n_1 - 1} \times \frac{n_2 - 1}{\Sigma(X_2 - \bar{X}_2)^2}$$

where X_1 and X_2 are values of the variable in Samples 1 and 2 respectively,

$\bar{X}_1$ and $\bar{X}_2$ are the means for Samples 1 and 2 respectively,

n_1 and n_2 are the numbers of observations in Samples 1 and 2 respectively.

100

If the samples were identical, this ratio would be equal to one but, in general, there is likely to be some difference between the variances and it is customary to arrange that the ratio is greater than (rather than less than) one. The ratio is represented by F and, in a statistical test, it is necessary to determine how far F differs from unity, which is the value it would have if the null hypothesis were true. F depends on the number of degrees of freedom of the two samples and the values for 0.05 and 0.01 significance levels can be read from tables in order to determine the degree of significance of a calculated value.

Example Suppose that, for a group of 21 students who were given reading lists, the standard deviation of the number of hours per week spent in the library is 3 and, for a group of 16 students who were not given reading lists, the standard deviation of the number of hours per week spent in the library is 2.

The null hypothesis to be investigated is that there is no significant difference between the variances of the two groups.

$$F = \frac{s_1^2}{s_2^2}$$

$$= \frac{3^2}{2^2}$$

$$= 2.25$$

From the F table (Appendix 6) for the 0.01 significance level and 20 degrees of freedom for s_1 and 15 degrees of freedom for s_2, the value of F is 3.37. For the 0.05 significance level and the same degrees of freedom, the value of F is 2.33. Since the calculated value of F is less than either of these values, it indicates that there is no significant difference between the variance for the two samples. The null hypothesis is accepted and the provision of reading lists would be deemed not to have any appreciable effect on the variability of time spent in the library.

Examples

7.1 The mean number of books per shelf in a section of a library is 24.4. A random sample of 36 shelves carry a mean number of 25.2 books with a standard deviation of 1.6. Is the information gained from the sample representative of the whole population?

7.2 A national authority is organized in a number of areas. The number of users served per member of library staff in the various areas is:

150.0 108.6 143.0 77.8 66.7 143.0 246.0 128.0

Assuming the recommended user/library-staff ratio is 100:1, perform a *t*-test to determine whether the average provision of library staff in the authority in question differs significantly from the recommended norm.

7.3 Over a whole year of 52 weeks, the number of issues from a library was 30,000. In 10 weeks during the winter, the number of issues per week were found to be:

650 693 750 726 804 740 735 751 687 762

Perform a *t*-test to determine whether the demand for books is significantly greater or less during the winter.

7.4 When the mean price of a paperback was 50p, a random sample of paperbacks containing colour plates cost (in pounds):

1.25 0.55 1.05 0.50 0.75 0.85

Perform a *t*-test to determine whether the illustrated paperbacks were significantly more expensive than paperbacks in general.

7.5 The number of junior non-fiction books borrowed on a random sample of days in August were:

51	39	40
38	24	37
50	32	27
52	29	56
43	27	44

The mean number of daily borrowings over the whole year was 46.58. Is the demand for such books in August significantly greater or less than average?

7.6 In a citation study, 12 periodicals concerned with economics were cited the following number of times:

33 25 23 19 15 14 13 12 10 9 8 7

What is the mean number of citations per periodical in the sample? Does it differ significantly from the mean number of citations of all periodicals investigated which was 14.283?

7.7 If the online connect times for a random sample of searches carried out by a particular user are (in minutes):

22 13 17 14 15 18 19 14 17 20 21 13 15 18 17

. . . does the user appear to take significantly more or less time

102

than the 15 minutes which has been quoted as a mean connect time for such searching?

7.8 The mean price for all books for young people in 1959 was 11.402 shillings. The prices of a random sample of non-fiction books in that year were (in shillings):

$3\frac{1}{2}$ $10\frac{1}{2}$ $10\frac{1}{2}$ $10\frac{1}{2}$ $10\frac{1}{2}$ 28 28 $10\frac{1}{2}$ $10\frac{1}{2}$ $10\frac{1}{2}$
$9\frac{1}{2}$ $10\frac{1}{2}$ $9\frac{1}{2}$ 15 $10\frac{1}{2}$ $12\frac{1}{2}$ $7\frac{1}{2}$ $10\frac{1}{2}$ $10\frac{1}{2}$ 6

Does the mean price of non-fiction differ significantly from the mean price for all books?

7.9 A random sample of 10 shelves of geography books had a mean number of 27.3 books per shelf and a standard deviation of 3.16. A random sample of 10 shelves of books on production had a mean number of 32.0 books per shelf and a standard deviation of 6.04. Use a t-test to decide if the number of geography books per shelf is significantly different from the number of books per shelf on production.

7.10 The number of issues of junior non-fiction on a random sample of days in May and November were:

May	Nov	May	Nov
36	34	37	78
28	89	97	89
32	22	37	34
39	44	33	22
27	49	114	33
114	33	35	17

Does there appear to be a significant difference in demand between the two months?

7.11 Using the data of Example 7.10, determine the F ratio to find if the dispersion of issues of junior non-fiction in May is significantly different from that in November.

7.12 Using the data of Example 7.9, determine the F ratio to find if the dispersion of thickness of geography books differs significantly from that of books on production.

Part II

QUALITATIVE DATA

Chapter 8

PRESENTATION OF QUALITATIVE DATA

As with quantitative data, there is a number of possible ways of presenting qualitative data, depending on the nature of the data and the type of information that it is required to convey.

The raw data may simply be tabulated as shown in Figure 8.1 which gives an analysis by country of publication of the primary document of the abstracts contained in an issue of three abstracts journals in 1971.

Country	Computer and control abstracts July 1971	Lead abstracts 1971	Sociological abstracts July 1971
Benelux	42	34	22
France	55	7	76
Germany	162	37	14
Great Britain	310	147	24
USA	966	265	552
USSR	191	37	42
Other	265	79	239
Total	1991	606	969

Figure 8.1: Analysis of abstracts in three abstracting journals according to country of publication of primary document

Each abstract observed was allocated to the appropriate country category and did not involve a counting operation. The data are therefore qualitative.

However, although all the available information is included in the table, it is not easily and quickly absorbed by the reader. A reordering of the data may aid its assimilation — as shown in Figure 8.2.

107

Country	Computer and control abstracts July 1971	Lead abstracts 1971	Sociological abstracts July 1971
USA	966	265	552
Great Britain	310	147	24
Other	265	79	239
USSR	191	37	42
Germany	162	37	14
France	55	7	76
Benelux	42	34	22
Total	1991	606	969

Figure 8.2: Analysis of abstracts in three abstracting journals according to country of publication of primary document

In Figure 8.2, the data have been arranged in descending numerical order of number of abstracts in *Computer and control abstracts* rather than in alphabetical order of country as they were in Figure 8.1. It is now much clearer that there is a greater similarity of pattern of output between the two technological services than between either of those and the *Sociological abstracts*. The comparative paucity of sociological literature from Great Britain and of literature on lead from France stands out — as does the high proportion of sociological literature coming from France and from various other countries not specifically listed.

When larger numbers are involved, even arranging data in numerical order does not necessarily achieve the clarity desired. Such is the case with the data on book issues from a number of libraries shown in Figure 8.3.

Library	Year 1	Year 2
A	771,367	748,375
B	725,839	705,424
C	529,692	626,708
D	490,371	549,647
E	463,317	469,893
F	436,604	477,879
G	428,796	412,352

Figure 8.3: Book issues from a number of libraries

It is difficult to absorb and remember such large numbers and Ehrenberg discusses the usefulness of rounding numbers to two significant figures. Admittedly, such a procedure loses a degree of accuracy provided in the raw data but it is questionable as to whether that degree of accuracy is always necessary. By rounding the figures in Figure 8.3, the more easily assimilated tabulation of Figure 8.4 is obtained.

Library	Year 1	Year 2
A	77	75
B	73	71
C	53	63
D	49	55
E	46	47
F	44	48
G	43	41

Figure 8.4: Book issues from a number of libraries (10,000s)

None of the tabulations discussed so far provides obvious comparisons of the relative proportions of the data given. For example, it is difficult to see at a glance from Figure 8.1 or Figure 8.2 what proportion of the total numbers of abstracts in (say) *Computer and control abstracts* pertain to a particular country. A consequence of this is that the three abstracting services cannot easily be compared from the point of view of the relative quantities of literature from the various countries. If a basis for comparison is required, it can be achieved by converting the figures to percentages of the totals. Thus, the proportion of German documents abstracted in *Computer and control abstracts* in July 1971 is $\frac{162}{1991}$ and this is converted to a percentage by multiplying by 100:

$$\frac{162}{1991} \times 100 = 8.14\%$$

If this computation is carried out on all of the numbers in Figure 8.1, a similar tabulation is produced, but the total in each column is 100 as shown in Figure 8.5. Again, a reordering and/or a rounding of the numbers will aid assimilation.

There is now a basis for comparisons to be made between the three columns and it is clearly apparent, for example, that the proportion of American documents covered in the issue of *Lead abstracts* is only slightly less than the proportion of American documents covered in the

Country	Computer and control abstracts July 1971	Lead abstracts 1971	Sociological abstracts July 1971
Benelux	2.11	5.61	2.27
France	2.76	1.16	7.85
Germany	8.14	6.10	1.45
Great Britain	15.57	24.26	2.48
USA	48.52	43.73	56.97
USSR	9.59	6.10	4.33
Other	13.31	13.04	24.65
Total	100	100	100

Figure 8.5: Data from Figure 8.1 shown in the form of percentages

issue of *Computer and control abstracts* (43.73% as compared with 48.52%).

It should be noted, however, that the actual number of American documents covered in the issue of *Lead abstracts* cannot be determined from Figure 8.5 unless the total number of abstracts in the issue (ie 606) is also quoted. Given that information, the number of American documents can be calculated as follows:

$$\frac{43.73}{100} \times \frac{606}{1} = 265$$

Close scrutiny of tabulated data will thus provide a picture of the subject they represent, but some form of pictorial presentation will enable the data to be read and interpreted even more readily.

The *column chart* consists of a series of vertically elongated rectangles, each representing by its length the magnitude of the item to which it relates. Figure 8.6 is a column chart showing how the data of Figure 8.1 relating to *Computer and control abstracts* is represented by a set of columns, one for each country. The height of any column can be read from the scale on the left hand side.

The eight columns of Figure 8.6 may be amalgamated so that the information is represented by a single column with subdivisions to represent those portions of the total which relate to the individual countries. If the same procedure is carried out on each of the sets of numbers in Figure 8.1, the three abstracts bulletins can be represented by a single column chart from which comparisons can be made (Figure 8.7).

110

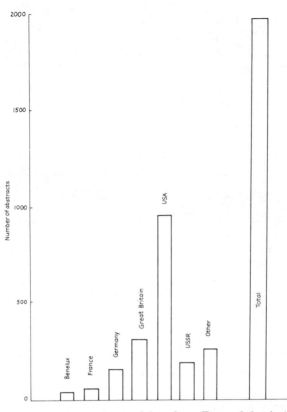

Figure 8.6: Column chart of data from Figure 8.1 relating to
Computer and control abstracts

Whilst the column chart presents the raw data clearly for quick perusal, precise figures cannot be read off unless it is plotted on a large scale on fine-mesh graph paper. Also, the problem of making comparisons between the relative coverages by country in the three abstracts journals still remains. However, the latter problem can be overcome by using a 100% *column chart* as illustrated in Figure 8.8, which represents the computed data of Figure 8.5. The actual number of abstracts may usefully be recorded on the chart as shown at the tops of the respective columns.

If other factors are to be taken into consideration, the relevant data may conveniently be displayed in a *grouped column chart*. For

111

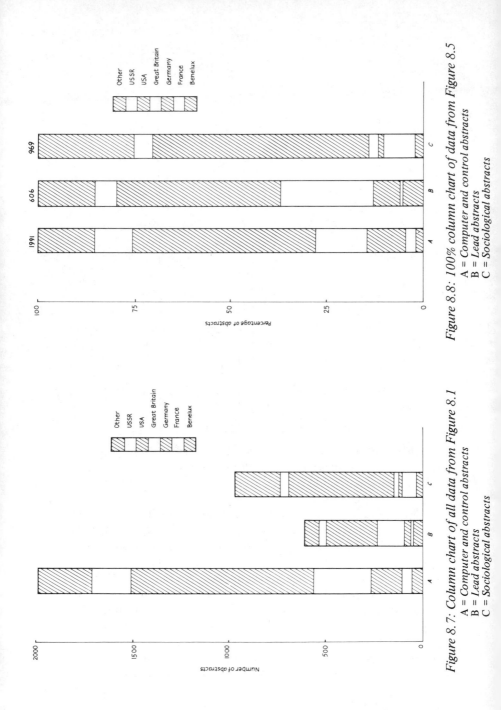

Figure 8.8: 100% column chart of data from Figure 8.5
A = *Computer and control abstracts*
B = *Lead abstracts*
C = *Sociological abstracts*

Figure 8.7: Column chart of all data from Figure 8.1
A = *Computer and control abstracts*
B = *Lead abstracts*
C = *Sociological abstracts*

example, in addition to comparing the three different abstracts journals, it may be of interest to investigate how the distribution by country varied with time. In this case, for each abstract journal, there will be a group of columns, each column representing the data for a specified year. Figure 8.9 is such a chart, grouping the data for each abstract journal for the years 1970, 1971, and 1972. It will be appreciated that the chart of Figure 8.9 is comparable with Figure 8.7, but there is no reason why a grouped column chart should not be of the 100% type comparable with Figure 8.8.

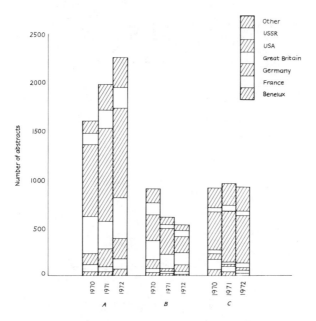

Figure 8.9: Grouped column chart
A = *Computer and control abstracts*
B = *Lead abstracts*
C = *Sociological abstracts*

Another variation with these data would be for each group to relate to a year and the three columns within each group to relate to the three abstracting journals.

A similar type of chart to the column chart is the *bar chart*, the only

113

difference being that, in the bar chart, the data are represented by a horizontal bar instead of by the vertical column of the column chart. The choice between the two is, to a great extent, a matter of personal preference, although the labelling of the whole or part of the data may be done more conveniently on bars than on columns. Figure 8.10 is a bar chart showing the same data as the column chart of Figure 8.7. The bar for *Computers and control abstracts* shows how the subdivisions of the bar may be labelled – if space permits – instead of using a key.

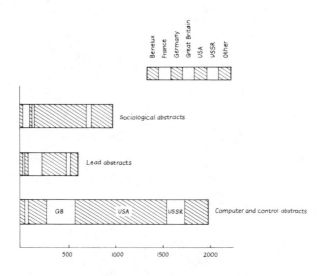

Figure 8.10: Bar chart of data from Figure 8.1

In presenting the data in column and bar charts, the subdivisions have been kept in alphabetical order of the name of the country. However, in practice, careful consideration would be given to the readers' expected approach, and the data would be presented accordingly. For example, it may be more usefully presented in decreasing order of magnitude of the subdivisions. The column chart would then appear as in Figure 8.11. Whilst a comparison between the breakdowns of the three sets of abstracts is not now so straightforward, the relative coverages of the various countries in each abstract journal is more obvious.

The *pie chart* is another way of presenting data, the subdivisions of

114

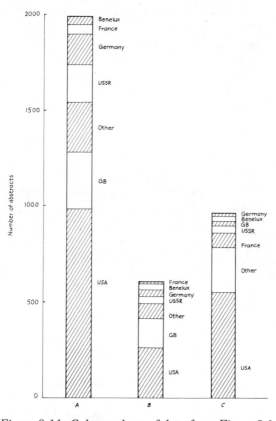

Figure 8.11: Column chart of data from Figure 8.1
A = *Computer and control abstracts*
B = *Lead abstracts*
C = *Sociological abstracts*

data being represented pictorially, in this case as the areas of the sectional portions of a circular pie. The area of the sector of a circle is proportional to the angle subtended at the centre, and the whole angle at the centre is 360°. Therefore, the angles at the centres of the various sectors are in the same proportions as the sizes of the subdivisions of data, and the first step in constructing a pie chart is to convert the data into degrees which, when totalled, amount to 360°. Figure 8.12 shows the data for *Computer and control abstracts* from Figure 8.1 dealt with in this way, the figure for Benelux, for example, being calculated thus:

$$\frac{42}{1991} \times 360° = 7.6°$$

115

Country	Number of abstracts	Degrees
Benelux	42	7.6
France	55	9.9
Germany	162	29.3
Great Britain	310	56.1
USA	966	174.7
USSR	191	34.5
Other	265	47.9
Total	1991	360.0

Figure 8.12: Analysis of abstracts in **Computer and control abstracts**, *July 1971, together with angles for pie chart*

The pie chart can now be drawn with radii spaced apart by the angles shown in Figure 8.12. The chart is shown in Figure 8.13

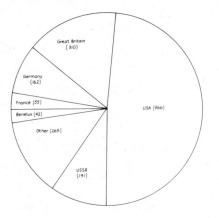

Figure 8.13: Pie chart of abstracts in **Computer and control abstracts**, *July 1971, according to country of publication of primary document*

It is helpful if the actual number of items in each category is recorded on the chart as shown.

It might usefully be noted that graph paper is obtainable on which a circle is divided into one hundred equal sectors. Hence, magnitudes in the form of percentages can be plotted directly to produce a pie diagram.

116

Examples

Represent the following sets of data in appropriate tables and/or diagrams.

8.1 A library contains the number of shelves of books on various languages as shown in the following table:

Subject	No of shelves
French	78
German	47
Russian	20
Spanish	30

8.2 The following table shows the numbers of periodical articles, patent specifications and other publications abstracted in three issues of each of *Copper abstracts, Lead abstracts* and *Zinc abstracts:*

	Periodical articles	Patent specs	Other publications
Copper abstracts: January 1963	51	0	5
Lead abstracts: January 1963	32	5	5
Zinc abstracts: January 1963	82	0	12
Copper abstracts: January 1966	60	2	12
Lead abstracts: January 1966	52	5	6
Zinc abstracts: January 1966	85	10	23
Copper abstracts: No 1 1970	84	8	13
Lead abstracts: January 1970	71	17	6
Zinc abstracts: January 1970	116	22	24

8.3 The photocopying statistics for a library are:

Catalogue reproduction	16,110
Official library work	65,350
Inter-library loan	2,600
Copying for readers	43,540

8.4 The photocopying statistics for four sections of a large library are:

	Section A	Section B	Section C	Section D
Catalogue reproduction	16110	3640	0	3400
Official library work	63350	11360	3080	5500
Inter-library loan	2600	1090	560	250
Copying for readers	43540	58040	1980	0

8.5   A library authority divided its budget as follows:

                   Staff   60%
                   Books 23%
                   Other 17%

8.6   The number of citations noted for given years in different subject fields were:

	1950	1960	1970
Sociology	330	414	547
Economics	299	393	295
Politics	115	357	137
Psychology	329	452	258

8.7   An estimate in 1969 of the cost per search (in £s) of performing searches on a computer was:

Development	2.03
Data preparation	2.18
Hardware	1.80
Computer time	0.60
Question formulation	1.40
Printing	1.00

8.8   Annual totals of issues from a library were:

Year	Non-fiction	Fiction	Junior	Total
1969	5857	37120	9166	52143
1970	5492	35597	6752	47841
1971	6985	38682	7615	53282
1972	7446	38192	8392	54030
1973	5594	35342	11282	52318
1974	5430	37741	13351	56522
1975	5391	38480	11433	55304
1976	5395	35837	7465	48697
1977	5588	38304	10535	54427
1978	5761	41001	9698	56460

8.9   Expenditure (£000s) by a library authority in each of four years was broken down as follows:

Year	Staff	Books	Other
1974/75	550	230	150
1975/76	720	260	215
1976/77	790	300	210
1977/78	830	320	230

Chapter 9

CHI-SQUARED TEST

Many annual reports of libraries contain a wealth of statistical data relating to the year under review. They cover such topics as book stock, population served, number of staff, expenditure under various heads, number of books issued etc. Very often, for comparison, corresponding figures are given for the previous year. For example, in a university library, the number of overnight loans recorded were:

$$\text{Overnight loans} \quad \frac{1971/2}{1456} \quad \frac{1972/3}{1656}$$

How satisfying is it to see an increase in the number of overnight loans? Are students working harder in the evenings?

A *chi-squared* test is used for assessing such qualitative data — to determine whether or not the difference between the two sets of figures is significant or purely a matter of chance.

The first step is to state a null hypothesis which is that there is no real difference between the number of overnight loans in the two years apart from chance variation. The alternative is that there is a difference between the number of overnight loans in the two years that cannot reasonably be accounted for by chance.

If the null hypothesis is correct, we could reasonably expect the total number of loans in the two years to be equally divided between them. Hence, in both 1971/2 and 1972/3, we would expect the number of loans to be:

$$\frac{1456 + 1656}{2}$$

ie 1556

To recapitulate, we now have the actual data recorded (to be called the 'observed frequency' — f_o) and the data that would be expected if

119

the null hypothesis were true (to be called the 'expected frequency' $-f_e$), thus:

	1971/2	1972/3
Observed frequency (f_o)	1456	1656
Expected frequency (f_e)	1556	1556

The differences (or *discrepancies*) between the observed and expected frequencies are:

	1971/2	1972/3
Discrepancy ($f_o - f_e$)	−100	+100

Chi-squared for the data in question can now be calculated from the expression:

$$\chi^2 = \sum \frac{(f_o - f_e)^2}{f_e}$$

ie
$$\chi^2 = \frac{(-100)^2}{1556} + \frac{(+100)^2}{1556}$$

$$= 6.427 + 6.427$$

$$= 12.854$$

This calculated value of χ^2 is compared with the sampling distribution of χ^2 in the manner described in Chapter 7. The test is a two-tailed test since it would be of interest to know if the number of overnight loans in 1972/3 is significantly greater or significantly less than in 1971/2.

The number of degrees of freedom is one less than the number of categories of observation, ie one degree of freedom in this example.

It will be seen from the χ^2 distribution (Appendix 7) that, for one degree of freedom and a two-tailed test, the 0.05 significance level is 3.841 and the 0.01 significance level is 6.635. Since the calculated value of χ^2 (12.854) is greater than either of these figures, it is highly significant and therefore the null hypothesis is rejected. The number of overnight loans was indeed appreciably greater in 1972/3 than it was in 1971/2.

However, further scrutiny of the reported statistics shows that the number of registered users of the library changed:

	1971/2	1972/3
Number of registered users	7237	8456

Over the two years, there was a total of 3112 loans (ie 1456 + 1656) and a total of 15,693 users. Therefore, the number of loans that we might expect the 7237 users in 1971/2 to have requested would be:

$$\frac{7237}{15693} \times 3112$$

ie 1435

Similarly, the number of loans that we might expect the 8456 users in 1972/3 to have requested would be:

$$\frac{8456}{15,693} \times 3112$$

ie 1677

That being the case, the observed and expected frequencies and discrepancies would be:

	1971/2	1972/3
Observed frequency	1456	1656
Expected frequency	1435	1677
Discrepancy	+21	−21

Chi-squared will now be:

$$\chi^2 = \frac{(+21)^2}{1435} + \frac{(-21)^2}{1677}$$

$$= 0.307 + 0.263$$

$$= 0.57$$

The number of degrees of freedom is still one, the 0.05 significance level is 3.841 and the 0.01 significance level is 6.635. The calculated value of χ^2 is less than either of these values and therefore it is not significant and we should confirm the null hypothesis that there is no significant difference between the overnight loans in the two years in question when the change in number of registered users is taken into consideration.

In the above examples, each observation of a loan was allocated to only one category — either to 1971/2 or to 1972/3. Often, observations are made, each of which is allocated to two categories as is the case with the data in Figure 8.1. Each abstract observed was allocated firstly in accordance with the abstract journal from which it was taken and secondly in accordance with the country of publication of the primary document. Such data can be presented in the form of a *contingency table*. This is a tabulation showing the relationships between the observed frequencies of attributes contingent upon each other. Some of the data from Figure 8.1 are shown in the contingency table of Figure 9.1.

	USA	Rest of world	Total
Computer and control abstracts	966	1025	1991
Lead abstracts	265	341	606
Total	1231	1366	2597

Figure 9.1: 2 × 2 contingency table of observed frequencies (f_o)

The table is known as a '2 × 2 contingency table' since, for each of the two abstracts journals, observations were made on the two attributes, viz 'USA' and 'Rest of world'.

Since there are 1991 abstracts in *Computer and control abstracts* out of a total of 2597 abstracts in both journals together, and there are 1231 abstracts of American documents altogether, one might expect the number of abstracts of American documents in *Computer and control abstracts* to be:

$$\frac{1991}{2597} \times 1231$$

ie 944

This is the expected frequency of abstracts of American publications in *Computer and control abstracts*. Similarly, three other expected frequencies can be found by using the general expression:

$$\text{Expected frequency} = \frac{\text{Row total} \times \text{Column total}}{\text{Grand total}}$$

'Row total' refers to the total for each row in the contingency table (ie 1991 and 606 in Figure 9.1). 'Column total' refers to the total for

122

each column in the contingency table (ie 1231 and 1366 in Figure 9.1), and 'Grand total' refers to the total of the row totals or of the column totals in the contingency table (ie 2597 in Figure 9.1).

When all the frequencies have been calculated, they can be tabulated as in Figure 9.2.

	USA	Rest of world	Total
Computer and control abstracts	944	1047	1991
Lead abstracts	287	319	606
Total	1231	1366	2597

Figure 9.2: Table of expected frequencies (f_e)

By subtracting each expected frequency from the corresponding observed frequency, the table of discrepancies — Figure 9.3 — is obtained.

	USA	Rest of world	Total
Computer and control abstracts	+22	−22	0
Lead abstracts	−22	+22	0
Total	0	0	0

Figure 9.3: Table of discrepancies ($f_o - f_e$)

Chi-squared can now be calculated:

$$\chi^2 = \frac{(+22)^2}{944} + \frac{(-22)^2}{1047} + \frac{(-22)^2}{287} + \frac{(+22)^2}{319}$$

$$= 4.18$$

The number of degrees of freedom of a system represented by a contingency table is found by multiplying (the number of columns − 1) by (the number of rows − 1). Therefore, for a 2 × 2 contingency table, the number of degrees of freedom is $(2 - 1) \times (2 - 1) = 1$. Assuming that we are interested to know whether the ratio of American to non-American documents is either greater in *Computer and control abstracts*

123

than in *Lead abstracts* or greater in *Lead abstracts* than in *Computer and control abstracts* — ie a two-tail situation — it will be seen from the χ^2 distribution that the calculated value of χ^2 is significant at the 0.05 level. So, there may be a significant difference between the two abstracting services from the point of view of their coverage of American documents relative to their coverage of documents published in the rest of the world.

Contingency tables are not limited to two rows and two columns of data. Figure 9.4 is an example of a 2 × 7 contingency table.

	Computer and control abstracts	Lead abstracts	Total
Benelux	42	34	76
France	55	7	62
Germany	162	37	199
Great Britain	310	147	457
USA	966	265	1231
USSR	191	37	228
Other	265	79	344
Total	1991	606	2597

Figure 9.4: 2 × 7 contingency table of observed frequencies

From these data, a χ^2 test can be performed to determine whether there is any significant difference between *Computer and control abstracts* and *Lead abstracts* from the point of view of the proportions of documents published in the various countries.

The expected frequencies, calculated from the observed frequencies as described above, are shown in Figure 9.5.

The discrepancies, derived from the observed and expected frequencies, are shown in Figure 9.6.

Chi-squared can now be calculated:

$$\chi^2 = \frac{(-16)^2}{58} + \frac{8^2}{47} + \frac{9^2}{153} + \frac{(-40)^2}{350} + \frac{22^2}{944} + \frac{16^2}{175} + \frac{1^2}{264} + \frac{16^2}{18}$$

$$+ \frac{(-8)^2}{15} + \frac{(-9)^2}{46} + \frac{40^2}{107} + \frac{(-22)^2}{287} + \frac{(-16)^2}{53} + \frac{(-1)^2}{80}$$

$$= 54.54$$

	Computer and control abstracts	Lead abstracts	Total
Benelux	58	18	76
France	47	15	62
Germany	153	46	199
Great Britain	350	107	457
USA	944	287	1231
USSR	175	53	228
Other	264	80	344
Total	1991	606	2597

Figure 9.5: 2 × 7 contingency table of expected frequencies

	Computer and control abstracts	Lead abstracts	Total
Benelux	−16	16	0
France	8	−8	0
Germany	9	−9	0
Great Britain	−40	40	0
USA	22	−22	0
USSR	16	−16	0
Other	1	−1	0
Total	0	0	0

Figure 9.6: 2 × 7 contingency table of discrepancies

The number of degrees of freedom in this example is $(7 - 1) \times (2 - 1)$, ie 6. When the calculated value of χ^2 (ie 54.54) is compared with the tables of the χ^2 distribution for 6 degrees of freedom, it is found to be much greater than χ^2 at either the 0.05 or the 0.01 levels (12.59 and 16.81 respectively). It lies in the region in which a null hypothesis must be rejected. Therefore, it must be concluded that there is a significant difference between the two abstracts journals and, because the calculated value of χ^2 is so large, the difference must be highly significant.

When performing a chi-squared test, care must be taken that the expected frequency in any 'cell' of the contingency table is not too small. A minimum expected frequency of 10 is recommended and, if it is found to be less, two or more categories should be combined, if possible, in order to exceed the minimum value. In the last example, any attempt to break down the 'Other' category would have resulted in several cells being too small.

Whilst an expected frequency of 10 is a recommended minimum, it is difficult to draw a hard and fast line and some investigators accept 5 as a minimum value. However, between 10 and 5, the validity of chi-squared calculated as described is questionable. For a 2 × 2 contingency table only, it is possible to modify the calculation of χ^2 by means of the *Yates' correction* should one or more of the expected frequencies lie between 5 and 10. The correction involves subtracting 0.5 from the discrepancy, thus:

$$\chi^2 = \sum \frac{(|f_o - f_e| - 0.5)^2}{f_e}$$

In this expression, $|f_o - f_e|$ means 'subtract the expected frequency from the observed frequency and ignore the minus sign if the answer is negative'. Thus:

$$|42 - 58| = +16$$
$$|55 - 47| = +8$$

Examples

9.1   The numbers of volumes sought by a library on inter-library loan that proved unobtainable were, in successive years, 113 and 164 respectively. Is this a significant increase?

9.2   At library A, 297 users are males and 643 are females. At library B, 413 users are males and 976 are females. Is there any significant difference between the male/female ratio at the two libraries?

9.3   In a survey of students reading newspapers, 50 were in Department A, 34 of whom read the newspaper to help their academic work. There were 40 students from Department B, 22 of whom read the newspaper to help their academic work. Is there any significant difference between the students from the two departments from the point of view of their utilization of newspapers?

9.4   In a volume of 'books for young people', for the 9-11 year olds, 68 books were written by men and 94 by women, and for the 14-16 year olds, 116 books were written by men and 28 by women. Is there any significant difference between the sex of the authors for the two age groups?

9.5 In an experiment, the number of citations in 1950 to references on Sociology was 330 and on Economics was 299. In 1960, the number of citations to references on Sociology was 414 and on Economics was 393. Is there any significant difference between the relative numbers of citations to Sociology and Economics in the two years investigated?

9.6 In an investigation of knowledge about British Library MARC records, the following responses were reported with reference to the statement that they include ERIC records:

	True	False	No response
1977/8	37	56	24
1978/9	24	44	30

Is the change in response significant?

9.7 The following are figures for borrowings of adult fiction and non-fiction books by residents from two areas:

	Fiction	Non-fiction
Area A	745	870
Area B	251	304

Is the pattern of demand from Area A significantly different from that from Area B?

9.8 In an investigation of information transfer, the following data were collected:

Work group	Face-to-face	Phone	Other
A	1008	269	708
B	409	194	497

Is there any significant difference between work groups A and B as far as the pattern of information transfer methods is concerned?

9.9 In a school of librarianship, there were 32 post-graduate students and 60 first degree students commenced courses. Five of the post-graduate students and 8 of the first degree students did not complete their courses. Is there any significant difference between the two groups of students?

Part III

QUALITATIVE/QUANTITATIVE DATA

Chapter 10

PRESENTATION OF QUALITATIVE/QUANTITATIVE DATA

When the observations involve two variables and one is quantitative whilst the other is qualitative, a good way to present the data is by means of a *line graph*. Such a graph may be used, for example, to show trends over a period of time since time is a qualitative variable. Figure 10.1 is a line graph showing how the number of abstracts in *Computer and control abstracts* varied over a period of years. When looking at a volume of abstracts, the volume was allocated to the year category — which is therefore qualitative, and the number of abstracts in the volume was counted — which is therefore quantitative.

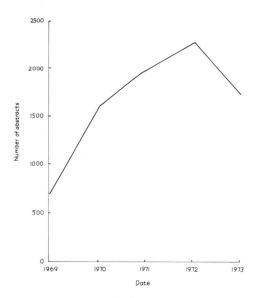

*Figure 10.1: Line graph showing the number of abstracts in
the July issues of Computer and control abstracts*

131

Care must be taken in the preparation of a line graph to ensure that the reader is not misled at a cursory glance. Figure 10.2 shows the effect of contracting the horizontal scale and suppressing the zero on the vertical scale to save space. It creates the impression of a much steeper rise than actually exists, starting from virtually zero.

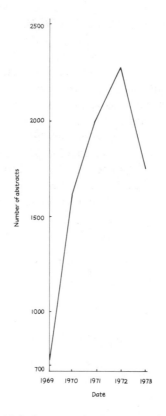

Figure 10.2: Line graph illustrating distortion

If it is necessary to condense an axis to save space, the zero must still be shown and the condensation can be indicated as illustrated in Figure 10.3.

When there is a rapid growth in magnitude of the quantitative variable, a linear scale is not necessarily the most suitable. Figure 10.4 shows the growth in number of scientific journals (in round numbers):

132

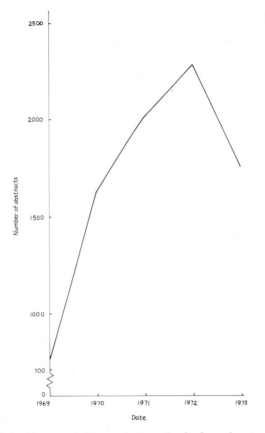

Figure 10.3: Line graph illustrating method of condensing the axis

Date	1700	1750	1800	1850	1900	1950
No of journals	8	10	90	1000	10,000	85,000

Figure 10.4: Growth in number of scientific journals

These data are plotted in Figure 10.5, from which the explosive growth in the number of scientific journals is clearly seen.

However, whilst actual numbers of journals may reasonably easily be read from the graph for more recent years, the change between the years 1700 and 1900 is so comparatively small that accurate informa-

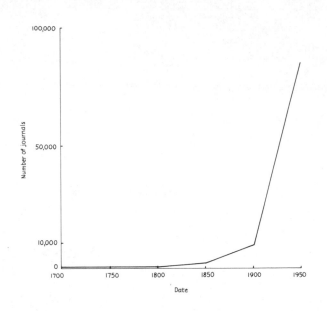

Figure 10.5: Line graph of growth in number of scientific journals

tion cannot be taken from the graph. In such circumstances, the quantitative variable should be plotted on a logarithmic scale. Figure 10.6 is a reproduction of Figure 10.4 with the addition of the logarithms of the numbers of journals taken from a table of logarithms.

Date	1700	1750	1800	1850	1900	1950
No of journals	8	10	90	1000	10,000	85,000
Log of no of journals	0.903	1.000	1.954	3.000	4.000	4.929

Figure 10.6: Growth in number of scientific journals

The logarithm of the number of journals is plotted against the date on what is known as a *semi-logarithmic graph* (Figure 10.7). Specially prepared semi-logarithmic graph paper can be purchased, which makes the task of preparing such graphs much simpler. From Figure 10.7, a reasonably accurate measure can be made of the number of journals for any date in the whole range.

More than one line graph may be drawn on one set of axes, using

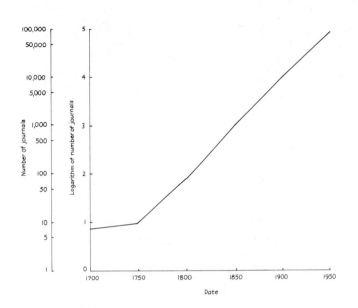

Figure 10.7: Semi-logarithmic graph of the growth of number of scientific journals

dotted or dashed lines if necessary to add clarity. Figure 10.8 includes line graphs to show the variation in number of documents published in the USA and Great Britain respectively, in addition to the graph showing the total number of abstracts in several issues of *Computer and control abstracts.*

Whilst the line graph clearly shows the trends of the several variables and the magnitudes of each can be read from the vertical scale, the relative magnitudes may be more clearly seen from a *surface graph.* In this type of graph, the magnitudes of the variables are represented by the spaces between the lines shown in Figures 10.9 and 10.10. The latter is known as a *100% surface graph* and is comparable with the 100% column chart of qualitative data (Figure 8.8). The 100% surface graph is used if only the relative sizes of the variables are of interest, whilst the surface graph of Figure 10.9 is used if the actual sizes of the variables are important. There are, of course, alternative orders in which the variables may be recorded, just as there is in the column chart, eg decreasing magnitude or alphabetical order of titles of variables.

135

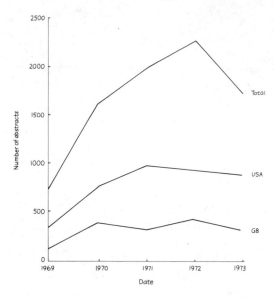

Figure 10.8: Line graph showing several variables

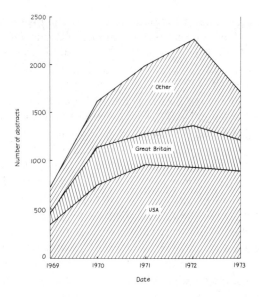

Figure 10.9: Surface graph

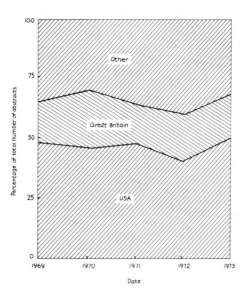

Figure 10.10: 100% surface graph

Examples

Represent the following sets of data in appropriate tables and/or diagrams:

10.1 The approximate total numbers of physics abstracts published by certain dates are:

Date	No of abstracts	Date	No of abstracts
1905	12,000	1930	73,000
1910	28,000	1935	92,000
1915	37,000	1940	125,000
1920	43,000	1945	135,000
1925	52,000	1950	175,000

10.2 The percentage increases in book prices and items purchased by a library in each of the ten years 1968-1978 as compared with 1967/68 were:

Date	Book prices	Items purchased
1967/68	0	0
1968/69	15	18
1969/70	37	9
1970/71	51	36
1971/72	60	32
1972/73	83	−18
1973/74	115	0
1974/75	159	0
1975/76	256	32
1976/77	350	24
1977/78	427	16

10.3 Expenditure (£000s) by a library authority in each of four years was broken down as follows:

Date	Staff	Books	Other
1974/75	550	230	150
1975/76	720	260	215
1976/77	790	300	210
1977/78	830	320	230

10.4 The Book Cost Index and the Retail Price Index for a number of years were:

	1974	1975	1976	1977	1978	1979
Book Cost Index	100	120.6	154.7	181.5	211.1	261.8
Retail Price Index	100	119.9	147.9	172.4	189.5	207.2

10.5 A bibliography of teenage fiction included the following number of titles for the years 1945-1958:

Year	No of titles	Year	No of titles
1945	1	1952	8
1946	5	1953	26
1947	6	1954	40
1948	6	1955	39
1949	19	1956	43
1950	8	1957	54
1951	13	1958	50

10.6 Monthly totals of book issues from a library were:

Month	Non-fiction	Fiction	Junior
Jan	465	3216	713
Feb	513	3215	686
Mar	425	3126	996
Apr	402	3101	642
May	436	3201	875
Jun	971	3826	2857
Jly	1334	5379	3293
Aug	1397	5809	2801
Sep	1248	5782	2450
Oct	1332	6754	2613
Nov	1047	5376	1906
Dec	594	4199	990

Chapter 11

INDEXES

When the value of a commodity varies from time to time, some measure is required to give an indication of the value at any given time. This is the purpose of an *index* which is a figure that relates the value at the time in question with the value at some reference date that is used as a basis for comparison.

A well-known example is the Index of Share Prices that shows how the buying price or selling price of shares on the Stock Market compares with the price on the date used as a basis. Another example is the Index of Retail Prices that compares the cost of a selection of household items with their cost on the date used as a basis.

The year used as a basis for comparison is known as the *base year* and it is usual to represent the value of the commodity in the base year by the figure 100.

Any year under consideration is known as the *given year*, in which the value of the same commodity is said to be the index for the given year.

For example, if the Index of Retail Prices is 140 in a given year, it means that the value of the selection of household items in that year is of magnitude 140 compared with a magnitude of 100 for the same selection of household items in the base year — showing that the value in the given year was 40% greater than in the base year. Thus:

$$\frac{\text{Value in given year}}{\text{Value in base year}} = \frac{140}{100}$$

So, in general terms:

$$\frac{\text{Value in given year}}{\text{Value in base year}} \times 100 = \text{Index for the given year}$$

Or, since the 'value' is directly related to the 'cost', the index, I, is given by:

140

$$I = \frac{\text{Cost in given year}}{\text{Cost in base year}} \times 100$$

Such an index can be used whenever we have any variable quantity that changes from time to time in order to give a measure of the magnitude of the variable compared with its magnitude at some earlier date of reference.

Suppose that the cost, in pence, of a paperback over a period of years was:

Year	1970	1971	1972	1973	1974	1975
Cost	25	30	35	40	45	50

Taking 1970 as the base year, the index for the cost of a paperback in 1971 would be $\frac{30}{25} \times 100$, ie 120.

Working out similarly the index for each of the subsequent years, we get:

Year	1970	1971	1972	1973	1974	1975
Index	100	120	140	160	180	200

When, as in this example, we are concerned with only a single commodity (ie paperbacks), little is gained by working out an index figure since the change over the years can be seen almost as clearly from the actual prices. However, the index does allow the percentage change to be seen more easily.

Simple aggregative index

If we are concerned with the change in overall value of several commo-. dities (as with retail prices), the index is essential. Suppose that a library purchases books, periodicals and newspapers. Typical figures (in pence) might be:

	Base year	Given year	Index
Book	200	450	$\frac{450}{200} \times 100 \ (= 225)$
Periodical	30	50	$\frac{50}{30} \times 100 \ (= 167)$
Newspaper	5	10	$\frac{10}{5} \times 100 \ (= 200)$

The average index, taking into consideration all items, will be:

$$\frac{\frac{450}{200} \times 100 + \frac{50}{30} \times 100 + \frac{10}{5} \times 100}{3} \quad \dots (1)$$

141

$$= \frac{225 + 167 + 200}{3}$$

$$= \tfrac{592}{3}$$

$$= 197$$

So, the overall cost of a book, a periodical and a newspaper was 197 in the given year compared with 100 in the base year — although the index for any individual item can be quite different.

The expression for the index at (1) can be rewritten as:

$$\frac{(\tfrac{450}{200} + \tfrac{50}{30} + \tfrac{10}{5}) \times 100}{3}$$

If we let the price of any item in the base year be represented by p_o and the price of any item in the given year be p_n, the index for that item can be written as $\frac{p_n}{p_o} \times 100$, and the overall index can be written as:

$$I = \frac{\sum \frac{p_n}{p_o} \times 100}{k}$$

where k is the number of commodities.

However, it can be rather tedious working out $\frac{p_n}{p_o}$ for each commodity and then summing. It is much easier to add the costs of the commodities in the base year and in the given year respectively. Hence, an index can be calculated by using the expression:

$$I = \frac{\Sigma p_n}{\Sigma p_o} \times 100$$

The index found by this procedure is known as a *simple aggregative index*.

Using the figures for the costs of a book, a periodical and a newspaper given above, the simple aggregative index for the given year will be found to be:

$$I = \frac{450 + 50 + 10}{200 + 30 + 5} \times 100$$

$$= \tfrac{510}{235} \times 100$$

$$= 217$$

The actual value of the index obviously depends on the method of calculation but, so long as the same procedure is always used, a consistent result will be achieved.

Weighted aggregative index

In fact, although the simple aggregative index is easy to calculate, it is not a very satisfactory index because its value depends on the units in which prices are quoted. For example, if the periodical cost were an annual subscription and not a cost per issue as was previously assumed, the table would be (assuming the periodical to be monthly):

	Base year	Given year
Book	200	450
Periodical	360	600
Newspaper	5	10

The simple aggregative index would now be:

$$I = \frac{450 + 600 + 10}{200 + 360 + 5} \times 100$$

$$= \frac{1060}{565} \times 100$$

$$= 187.6$$

A more satisfactory index is the weighted aggregative index. In this case, the cost of each commodity is weighted in some logical way. In our example, the weighting factor would be the number of items purchased annually. For example:

Number of books   50

Number of periodical titles (monthly) 40
    Hence, total number of issues of periodicals $40 \times 12 = 480$

Number of daily newspapers (Mon-Sat) 2
    Hence, total number of newspapers $2 \times 6 \times 52 = 624$

If we let the quantity of any item in the base year be represented by q_o, the available data can now be tabulated as follows:

	q_o	p_o	p_n
Books	50	200	450
Periodicals	480	30	50
Newspapers	624	5	10

143

$$= I = \frac{\left(p_n \times q_o\right) + \left(p_n \times q_o\right) + \left(p_n \times q_o\right)}{\left(450 \times 50\right) + \left(50 \times 480\right) + \left(10 \times 624\right)}$$

The weighted aggregative index is calculated by the following expression:

$$I = \frac{\Sigma p_n q_o}{\Sigma p_o q_o} \times 100$$

ie $\qquad I = \frac{(450 \times 50) + (50 \times 480) + (10 \times 624)}{(200 \times 50) + (30 \times 480) + (5 \times 624)} \times 100$

$$= \frac{52740}{27520} \times 100$$

$$= 191.6$$

Since the weights in this calculation were the quantities purchased in the base year, the procedure is known as 'Base year weighting'. The index compares what it would cost in the given year to buy the quantity of goods that actually were bought in the base year with what it cost in the base year to buy those goods.

Alternatively, we can use 'Current year weighting'. This is an analagous procedure but uses the quantities pertaining to the given year (q_n) instead of those for the base year. The index is now:

$$I = \frac{\Sigma p_n q_n}{\Sigma p_o q_n} \times 100$$

In this case, the index compares what it costs to buy a quantity of goods in the given year with what it would have cost to buy the same quantity of goods in the base year.

Suppose the data were:

	p_o	p_n	q_n
Books	200	450	60
Periodicals	30	50	360
Newspapers	5	10	624

Then:

$$I = \frac{(450 \times 60) + (50 \times 360) + (10 \times 624)}{(200 \times 60) + (30 \times 360) + (5 \times 624)} \times 100$$

$$= \frac{51240}{25920} \times 100$$

$$= 197.7$$

Again, it will be noted that the index depends on its method of calculation and therefore it should be made clear what it represents.

Indexes are not restricted to questions of costs. For example, a library might be interested in the change in overall borrowing, whilst appreciating that different age-groups have different reading habits and constitute different proportions of the reading population.

Suppose:

$$p = \text{number of borrowings per year per reader}$$
$$q = \text{percentage of library users in age groups}$$

Age group	q_o	p_o	p_n
Under 15	10	50	80
15-25	30	150	250
25-50	20	100	100
50-	40	200	150

The simple aggregative index would be:

$$I = \frac{80 + 250 + 100 + 150}{50 + 150 + 100 + 200} \times 100$$

$$= \frac{580}{500} \times 100$$

$$= 116$$

The weighted aggregative index, with base year weighting, would be:

$$I = \frac{(80 \times 10) + (250 \times 30) + (100 \times 20) + (150 \times 40)}{(50 \times 10) + (150 \times 30) + (100 \times 20) + (200 \times 40)} \times 100$$

$$= \frac{16300}{15000} \times 100$$

$$= 108.7$$

That index shows that, if the numbers of readers in the various age groups were the same in the given year as in the base year, the number of borrowings was 8.7% higher in the given year than in the base year.

Chain base index
Instead of comparing any given year with the same specified base year, it is sometimes useful to have an index to show how the value of a

commodity has changed since the previous year. For example, the total numbers of issues of volumes of non-fiction by a library in a number of years were:

Year	1960	1961	1962	1963	1964
No of issues	8094	9288	8416	9271	8233

Then the values of the chain base index for each of the years from 1961 onwards are deduced as follows:

Year	Chain base index
1961	$\frac{9288}{8094} \times 100 = 114.75$
1962	$\frac{8416}{9288} \times 100 = 90.61$
1963	$\frac{9271}{8416} \times 100 = 110.16$
1964	$\frac{8233}{9271} \times 100 = 88.80$

Hence, in 1961, there were 14.75% more issues than in 1960, and in 1962, there were $(100 - 90.61)\%$, ie 9.39% fewer issues than in 1961 and so on.

In contrast, values of a simple index for the same data would be $(1960 = 100)$:

Year	Simple index
1960	100
1961	$\frac{9288}{8094} \times 100 = 114.75$
1962	$\frac{8416}{8094} \times 100 = 103.98$
1963	$\frac{9271}{8094} \times 100 = 114.54$
1964	$\frac{8233}{8094} \times 100 = 101.72$

Hence, in 1961, there were 14.75% more issues than in 1960 and in 1962 there were 3.98% more issues than in 1960 and so on.

Examples

11.1 The following data show the average costs (in pounds) of different types of document in a base year and in a given year:

	Base year	Given year
Books	1.50	3.50
Patents	0.30	0.50
Periodicals	2.40	4.80

(a) if, in the given year, a library buys 120 books, 2000 patent specifications and 75 periodicals, calculate (i) the simple aggregative index and (ii) the weighted aggregative index to show how the total cost in the given year compares with the total cost that would have been incurred in the base year if the same number of documents had been purchased;

(b) if, in the base year, the library had bought 100 books, 1500 patent specifications and 90 periodicals, calculate the weighted aggregative index to show, in comparison with the base year, the total cost in the given year of buying the same quantity of documents as were purchased in the base year.

11.2 If, in a base year, each loan of a record were charged at 5p, each cassette at 3p and each language record album at 10p, calculate a weighted aggregative index to represent the total income in a given year (compared with base year = 100) if the charges were raised to 7p, 5p and 12p and the number of loans are 236, 157 and 21 respectively. Would it have been better to raise charges to 6p, 6p and 15p respectively? If the language record albums are to be charged at 15p and records are to be charged at the same rate as cassettes, what would that rate be (to the nearest penny) if at least 60% overall increase compared with the base year is to be achieved?

11.3 The following data relate to the running expenses for a library's premises:

	Actual 1976/77	Estimated 1977/78	Probable 1977/78	Actual 1977/78
Repairs	14827	18600	18000	14206
Alterations	2400	2700	2700	3045
Fuel	36549	43900	50700	39456
Furniture	4535	2200	2200	1963
Rent	40290	44100	51700	51077

(a) Calculate simple aggregative indexes to show how:

(i) the total estimated expenditure

(ii) the probable expenditure

(iii) the actual expenditure

for 1977/78 compared with 1976/77 actual expenditure.

(b) What would be the estimated expenditure (to the nearest £) for 1978/79 for each of the five items if you allow a percentage increase on each actual 1977/78 expenditure equal to the overall actual percentage increase for 1977/78 compared with 1976/77?

(c) What is the simple aggregative index for 1978/79 estimated expenditure (1976/77 = 100)?

11.4 The expenditure of a library authority in a number of years was broken down as follows (in £000s):

	1974/75	1975/76	1976/77	1977/78
Staff	550	710	790	810
Books	230	260	300	330
Other	140	220	210	210

(a) Calculate a simple aggregative index for the total expenditure in each of the years 1975/76, 1976/77 and 1977/78 compared with the base year 1974/75.

(b) Is the percentage increase in expenditure on books between 1974/75 and 1977/78 greater or less than the percentage increase in total expenditure?

11.5 In a given year, the mean salary of the five members of a library staff was £4750; 2500 books were purchased at a mean price of £4.25, and services cost £6000.

(a) Determine the weighted aggregative index to show how the total expenditure in the given year compared with what it would have been in a base year when the mean salary was £4000, the mean cost of a book was £3.00 and services cost £5000.

(b) Is the simple aggregative index for the given year appreciably different from the weighted aggregative index?

11.6 Using the data of example 11.4, calculate the chain base indexes to show how expenditure on (a) staff and (b) books in 1975/76, 1976/77 and 1977/78 compared with the preceding years.

Chapter 12

TIME SERIES

Time series are concerned with quantities that vary over a period of time, eg the mean cost of a book; the number of items issued daily by a library; the number of abstracts on a given subject in a monthly publication; etc. The actual magnitudes of such quantities are likely to vary quite erratically but the long-term change, or *trend*, may be of interest.

Suppose that the values of a hypothetical variable for each of eleven successive years were:

$$4 \quad 8 \quad 7 \quad 9 \quad 10 \quad 8 \quad 13 \quad 16 \quad 15 \quad 13 \quad 14$$

These data can be represented diagrammatically in the form of a line graph sometimes known as a *historigram* (Figure 12.1).

Clearly, the data display a general upward trend with the passage of time but it would be useful to be able to indicate the trend concisely — as it is useful to represent the magnitudes of a collection of variables by quoting an average.

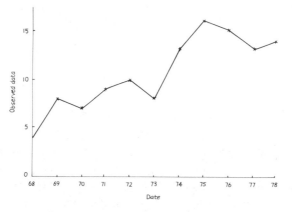

Figure 12.1: Historigram

As the trend in Figure 12.1 appears to be approximately linear, a straight line could be drawn through the points by visual inspection. However, there are more rigorous methods of determining the *trend line* which represents the average change in magnitude of the variable over the time investigated.

In the *method of semi-averages*, the values of the variable are divided into two halves. If there is an odd number of observations, the middle value is either omitted or included in both halves. The mean of each of the two sections of data is determined:

$$\frac{4 + 8 + 7 + 9 + 10}{5} \quad \text{and} \quad \frac{13 + 16 + 15 + 13 + 14}{5}$$

ie   7.6   and   14.2

These two mean values are plotted on the graph at the time intervals corresponding to the mid-points of the two halves. The two points so plotted are joined by a straight line which is extrapolated in either direction as far as the period of observation extends (Figure 12.2).

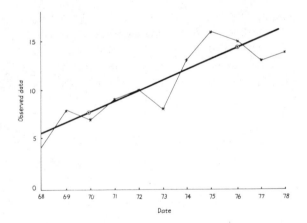

Figure 12.2: Historigram showing raw data and trend line

Whilst it is possible to forecast the value of the variable at a future date, it should be noted that it can be dangerous to extrapolate beyond the period for which data are available because the future trend cannot be foreseen. Whereas it may continue in the same straight line, it may suddenly increase or decrease owing to a variety of possible influences.

150

An alternative procedure for determining the trend line involves firstly dividing the data into three parts and then determining the medians of the first and third parts:

	First part	Second part	Third part
Raw data	4 8 7 9 /	10 8 13 /	16 15 13 14
Array	4 7 8 9		13 14 15 16
Median	7.5		14.5

The medians are plotted on the graph at the time intervals corresponding to the mid-points of the respective parts and are joined by a straight line. Next, the median for the complete set of data is determined:

Raw data	4	8	7	9	10	8	13	16	15	13	14
Array	4	7	8	8	9	10	13	13	14	15	16
Median						10					

This median is also plotted — at a time interval corresponding to the middle of the array. A line, parallel to the first line, is drawn through that point. The trend line is a line drawn parallel to, and between, the other two lines and one third of the way from the first towards the second (Figure 12.3).

The above methods of finding the trend line can be applied only when the trend is approximately linear. A trend line found by the method of semi-averages for the following data is shown in Figure 12.4:

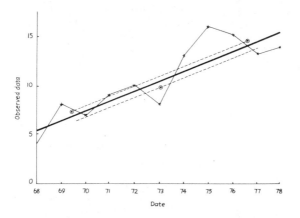

Figure 12.3: Historigram showing raw data and trend line

151

1 2 1 3 2 4 3 6 6 8 10

It will be apparent that the graph of the raw data rises above the trend line at each end and dips below it at the centre. The data display a distinct curvature.

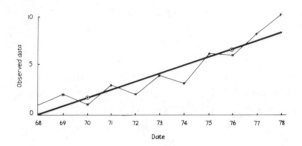

Figure 12.4: Non-linear data with attempt to draw trend line by the method of semi-averages

In such cases, it is necessary to find a *moving average*. A three-year moving average for the last set of data is found by the following steps:

1   Add together the first three numbers and divide by three, ie:

$$\frac{1 + 2 + 1}{3}$$

$$= 1.33$$

This is plotted against the same year as the middle of the three numbers.

2   Add together the second, third and fourth numbers and divide by three:

ie
$$\frac{2 + 1 + 3}{3}$$

$$= 2.00$$

This is again plotted against the same year as the middle of the three numbers.

3   Add together the third, fourth and fifth numbers and divide by three:

ie
$$\frac{1 + 3 + 2}{3}$$

$$= 2.00$$

152

And so on until all the data have been used. Figure 12.5 is a graph of the raw data on which is superimposed the trend line found by the above procedure.

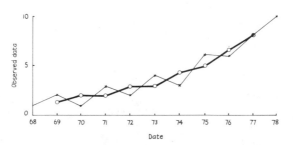

Figure 12.5: Non-linear data with trend line based on a three-point moving average

It will be seen that the trend line is a curve roughly following the curvature of the raw data. A drawback of the moving average will also be noted, viz it does not extend at each end as far as the raw data from which it is derived.

By following the same procedure but adding together five numbers at a time and dividing by five, a five-point moving average is found:

ie
$$\frac{1 + 2 + 1 + 3 + 2}{5}$$

$$= 1.8$$

$$\frac{2 + 1 + 3 + 2 + 4}{5}$$

$$= 2.4$$

And so on. The moving average is shown superimposed on the raw data in Figure 12.6. Note the smoother curve of the trend line in this case.

Whilst the trend line shows the long-term change in value of a variable, there are short-term changes which may also occur. These may be seasonal changes, as for example, book issues being greater in the winter than in the summer. They may be cyclical variations which constitute a pattern of change at regular intervals of time, for example, a peak of library use during the lunch period. Or they may be irregular events which may not be foreseen, such as a fall in the expected level of library use due to a breakdown of public transport or to inclement

153

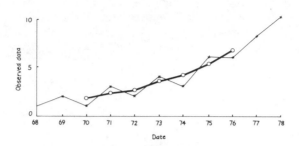

*Figure 12.6: Non-linear data with trend line based on a
five-point moving average*

weather conditions. When there is a regular pattern of variation, the order of moving average used to find the trend is determined by the number of observations within each cycle of the pattern. If the observations relate to three parts of a working day (morning, afternoon and evening), a three-point moving average is used. If the observations relate to a six-day working week, a six-point moving average is used and if observations relate to the four seasons of the year, a four-point moving average would be appropriate. Suppose some data for the winter, spring, summer and autumn seasons over a three year period are as shown in column three of Figure 12.7. A four-point moving average is shown in column four. It will be noted that the values of the moving average fall between seasons — as, for example, the value of 2.00 of the moving average falls between spring and summer of Year 1. It is convenient to find the average of each pair of values of the moving average and these values, shown in column five, now fall opposite to the seasons and can be plotted on a graph to show the trend (Figure 12.8). If the average of the moving average is subtracted from the raw data (ie column 5 — column 3), the deviations in column six are obtained. The deviations are plotted graphically in Figure 12.8 and show the seasonal variation separated from the trend.

As an example of the application of this type of analysis, assume that the data are a measure of the number of outside loans handled by a library and hence a measure of staff time required for that work. The rising trend line might indicate that, if the demand for loans continues to increase, an additional permanent member of staff may be justified. On the other hand, the seasonal variation would suggest that, irrespective of any long-term requirements, a seasonal redeployment of staff may be necessary. In the winter, some additional help may

154

Year	Season	Raw data	Moving average	Average of the moving average	Deviations
1	W	3			
	Sp	2			
			2.00		
	Su	1		2.125	−1.125
			2.25		
	A	2		2.375	−0.375
			2.50		
2	W	4		2.625	1.375
			2.75		
	Sp	3		3.000	0.0
			3.25		
	Su	2		3.500	−1.5
			3.75		
	A	4		4.000	0.0
			4.25		
3	W	6		4.500	1.5
			4.75		
	Sp	5		5.000	0.0
			5.25		
	Su	4			
	A	6			

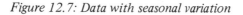

Figure 12.7: Data with seasonal variation

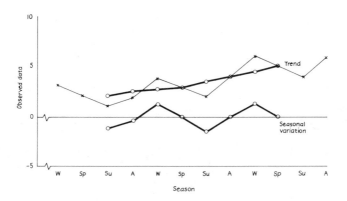

Figure 12.8: Raw data analysed into trend and seasonal variation

be needed to handle the above-average demand for loans, whilst in the summer, the staff may have time to spare to undertake other duties.

Referring again to Figure 12.7, it was not possible to subtract the moving average from the raw data and an average of the moving average had to be calculated in order to be able to find the deviation. This situation will occur whenever the number of observations in a cycle of the raw data is even. If the number of observations in a cycle is odd, the moving average can be subtracted directly from the raw data to obtain the deviation, making the intermediate step of finding an average of the moving average unnecessary. For example, the data in Figure 12.9 relate to the number of books issued in a library in the morning, afternoon and evening sessions on successive days and shows a three-point moving average:

Day	Session	Number of issues	Moving average	Deviation
1	M	20		
	A	25	18.33	6.67
	E	10	20.00	−10.00
2	M	25	21.00	4.00
	A	28	21.67	6.33
	E	12	22.00	−10.00
3	M	26	24.33	1.67
	A	35	24.67	10.33
	E	13		

Figure 12.9: Data on book issues in a library

Examples

12.1 The number of books issued in each of ten years (in thousands) were:

Year	No of issues
1	3.56
2	3.94
3	3.91
4	3.89
5	4.04
6	4.01
7	4.12
8	3.98
9	4.07
10	4.19

Work out a four-year moving average to show the trend of book issues. What percentage increase is there between the first and last values of the moving average and hence what is the mean annual percentage increase in number of issues?

12.2 The following are daily issues of junior non-fiction from a library:

Day	Week 1	Week 2	Week 3
M	39	30	17
Tu	14	33	31
W	21	18	20
Th	47	29	27
F	36	37	34
S	96	82	61

Calculate the moving average and the cyclical variation and sketch the graphs of the raw data, the moving average and the cyclical variation.

12.3 The cost (in pence) of an 'Agatha Christie' published by Fontana in a number of years was as follows:

Year	Cost	Year	Cost
1969	20	1974	35
1970	25	1975	45
1971	25	1976	60
1972	30	1977	65
1973	30	1978	75
		1979	80

Calculate a five-year moving average. From the moving average, determine the mean annual increase in cost between 1971 and 1973, between 1975 and 1977 and between 1971 and 1977.

12.4 US book production over a period of years was as follows:

Year	No of titles	Year	No of titles
1963	25784	1969	29579
1964	28451	1970	36071
1965	28595	1971	37692
1966	30050	1972	38053
1967	28762	1973	39951
1968	30387	1974	40846
		1975	39372

Calculate a five-year moving average and, from that, deduce the percentage increase in number of titles over a period of eight years.

12.5 A bibliography of teenage fiction included the following number of titles for the years 1945-1958:

Year	No of titles	Year	No of titles
1945	1	1952	8
1946	5	1953	26
1947	6	1954	40
1948	6	1955	39
1949	19	1956	43
1950	8	1957	54
1951	13	1958	50

Draw a rough sketch of these data and the trend line based on a five year moving average.

Chapter 13

ANALYSIS OF VARIANCE

The observed values of a quantitative variable form a frequency distribution and the spread of the values is measured by the standard deviation (σ) or variance (σ^2) of the distribution. For example, the number of books that can be stored on a shelf varies since it depends on the thickness of the books. As can be seen in Figure 1.3, an inspection of eighty shelves showed that the smallest number of books stored per shelf was 19 and the largest was 30.

The shelves to which those data relate were selected entirely at random, without consideration of the subject matter of the books. However, it could be hypothesized that the number of books that could be stored on a shelf depends on the subject field. In investigating this theory, shelves would be selected for observation and evaluated qualitatively according to subject field and quantitatively according to the number of books stored on the shelf. The results of such observations are tabulated in Figure 13.1. This twofold variation involving qualitative and quantitative data can be investigated by means of a process known as *analysis of variance*. A rigorous mathematical exposition is rather complex but the procedures to be followed are quite straightforward and will be described with reference to the data presented in Figure 13.1.

1   Add together the number of books for all the shelves in the three subject fields:

Number of geography books	= 273
Number of law books	= 241
Number of production engineering books	= 320
Total number of books	= 834

2   Square the total number of books and divide by the total number of shelves:

159

Geography	Law	Production engineering
25	21	36
30	21	23
30	33	30
29	23	30
25	16	32
23	26	33
28	26	23
33	28	34
25	26	43
25	21	36

*Figure 13.1: Number of books stored per shelf
in three subject fields*

ie
$$\frac{834^2}{30} = 23185.2$$

This is known as the 'correction factor'.

3   Square the number of books on each of the shelves and add these squares together:

$$25^2 + 21^2 + 36^2 + 30^2 + 21^2 \ldots + 25^2 + 21^2 + 36^2$$

$$= 24120$$

4   Subtract the correction factor from the result of step 3:

$$24120 - 23185.2 = 934.8$$

This is known as the 'total sum of the squares'.

5   Square the total number of books in each subject field and divide by the number of shelves observed in that subject field. Then add together the three figures obtained:

$$\frac{273^2}{10} + \frac{241^2}{10} + \frac{320^2}{10} = 7452.9 + 5808.1 + 10240.0$$

$$= 23501$$

6   Subtract the correction factor from the result of step 5:

$$23501 - 23185.2 = 315.8$$

Examples

13.1 A collection of documents was indexed in (a) a single-entry file and chain index and (b) a multiple-entry file and simple alphabetical index. The numbers of entries in the two files for a random sample of 12 documents were:

Single-entry	Multiple-entry
4	
3	4
4	3
4	6
5	4
4	6
3	6
3	4
3	3
5	4
5	6
2	6
	2

Does the number of entries per document appear to depend on the type of index?

13.2 Abstracts in *Economics abstracts* are written in English, French and German. The number of words in random samples of eight abstracts in each language were recorded as follows:

English	French	German
71	111	67
118	113	75
52	84	61
47	84	99
59	84	58
65	94	107
84	90	113
111	90	95

Does the length of abstract appear to depend on the language in which it is written?

This is known as the 'sum of squares between groups'.

7   Subtract the 'sum of squares between groups' from the 'total sum of the squares':

$$934.8 - 315.8 = 619.0$$

This is known as the 'sum of squares within groups'.

8   Determine the number of degrees of freedom (a) between groups and (b) within groups.

The number of degrees of freedom between groups is one less than the number of groups. Since there are three groups (Geography, Law and Production engineering), the number of degrees of freedom between groups is 2.

The number of degrees of freedom within groups is the sum of the number of degrees of freedom for each group. Since there are ten observations in each group, the number of degrees of freedom for each group is 9 and the number of degrees of freedom within groups is $9 + 9 + 9$, ie 27.

9   The data derived so far can be tabulated thus:

Source of variation	Sum of squares	Degrees of freedom	Mean sum of squares
Between groups	315.8	2	157.9
Within groups	619.0	27	22.93

The 'mean sum of squares' in the last column has been derived by dividing the 'sum of squares' (column 2) by 'degrees of freedom' (column 3).

10   Divide the larger mean sum of squares by the smaller mean sum of squares:

$$\frac{157.9}{22.93} = 6.89$$

This is the F ratio.

11   Compare the calculated value of F with the F distribution for 2 degrees of freedom in the numerator (v_n) and 27 degrees of freedom in the denominator (v_d). For these degrees of freedom, full tables of F (eg Pearson and Hartley) show that the 0.05 significance level 3.354 and the 0.01 significance level is 5.488.

Hence it must be concluded that there is a significant associati between the number of books per shelf and the subject field.

13.3 The numbers of junior books issued on sixteen full days in July and in January were:

July	January
54	61
61	46
44	50
50	17
50	45
54	31
59	20
54	54
22	37
58	38
45	30
30	42
25	58
29	44
24	58
38	38

Does the demand for books appear to differ between the summer and winter months?

Part IV

QUANTITATIVE/QUANTITATIVE DATA

Chapter 14

PRESENTATION OF QUANTITATIVE/QUANTITATIVE DATA

An investigation may involve the observation of two quantitative variables which are related in some way. For example, the purchase price of a book is likely to be related — among other factors — to the number of pages it contains. Data could be collected by counting the number of pages in each of a number of books looked at and counting the number of pound notes needed to purchase it. The data can be tabulated as in Figure 14.1.

Cost of book (£)	Number of pages
4.00	200
2.50	175
5.00	190
2.00	100
1.50	90
6.50	250
8.00	350

Figure 14.1: Cost and length of books

The usual graphical presentation of this type of data is known as a *scatter diagram.* In this type of diagram, one variable is measured from the horizontal axis, the other variable from the vertical axis. A mark at the point of intersection of the two measurements indicates an observation, showing the relationship between the two variables for each observation. Figure 14.2 shows the data from Figure 14.1, comparing the cost and length of books.

In drawing a scatter diagram, the scales should be chosen so that the spread of points horizontally is about the same as the spread of points vertically. The diagram is therefore roughly square in appearance. The

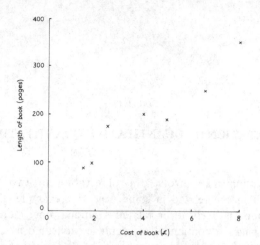

Figure 14.2: Scatter diagram of cost and length of books

way in which the two variables are related is clearly seen from the scatter diagram — a matter that will be discussed in the next chapter on correlation.

When the number of observations is large, the tabulated data may be presented more conveniently in a *correlation table*. The measurements of heights and widths of books on a library shelf are tabulated in Figure 14.3.

The data from Figure 14.3 are recorded in the correlation table of Figure 14.4. The table consists of a number of cells, each cell being associated with a particular value of one of the variables indicated across the top of the table and with a particular value of the other variable indicated down the side of the table. Conveniently, there should be between ten and twenty values of each variable.

If there are more than about twenty possible values of a variable, the data should be grouped. This has been done in Figure 14.5 which records the daily number of issues of fiction and non-fiction by a library. The smallest daily number of issues of fiction was 47 and the largest number was 295. Without grouping, 249 cells per column would be needed but, by collecting the data in groups of width 25, the number of cells per column has been limited to 11.

From the table, it can be seen, for example, that on six of the days, between 151 and 175 fiction books and between 26 and 30 non-fiction books were issued, that the median number of non-fiction issues is
168

Height	*Width*	*Height*	*Width*	*Height*	*Width*
8½	5½	8	5¼	7½	5
8¾	6	8	5½	7½	5¼
8¾	6	8	5¼	7½	5¼
6¾	4¼	8½	5¼	7	4¼
7¼	5¼	9¼	6	7½	5
7	4½	7½	5	7½	5
7½	5	7½	4¾	7	4¼
7¼	4¾	7½	5	7	4¼
6¾	4¼	7½	5	8¾	6
8¾	6	8½	5½	8½	5½
8¾	5½	7½	5	8¾	5½
7½	5	7½	5	8	5½
7	4¼	7¾	6	8¾	5½
8½	5½	7½	5	7	4¼
8½	5½	8¾	5½	9	5¾
7¼	5	8¾	5½	8½	5¼
8¾	5½	8¾	5½	8¾	6
7¼	4¾	8½	5½	8¾	5½
7½	5	7	4¾	8¾	6
8½	5¾	8¾	5½	7½	5¼
8	5¼	7½	5	8¾	5¾
7½	5	7½	5	9¼	6

Figure 14.3: The heights and widths (in inches) of a selection of books

		Heights of books (inches)											
		6¾	7	7¼	7½	7¾	8	8¼	8½	8¾	9	9¼	Totals
	4¼	2	5										7
	4½		1										1
	4¾		1	2	1								4
Widths of books (inches)	5			1	15				1				17
	5¼			1	3		3		2				9
	5½						2		5	9			16
	5¾								1	1	1		3
	6					1				6		2	9
	Totals	2	7	4	19	1	5	0	9	16	1	2	66

Figure 14.4: Correlation table of heights and widths of books

between 21 and 25 and that the modal group of fiction issues is 151-175. It is also apparent from the pattern of figures going from the top left of the table to the bottom right that the numbers of issues of fiction and non-fiction books increase or decrease together.

Number of non-fiction issues

Number of fiction issues	1-5	6-10	11-15	16-20	21-25	26-30	31-35	36-40	41-45	46-50	Totals
26-50	1	4									5
51-75	3	5	3								11
76-100		3	1	1							5
101-125		1	4	3	4	1	1				14
126-150				5	6	1	1				13
151-175			2	4	3	6	2	1			18
176-200				1	2	5	2	1			11
201-225				1	1	3	3	3			11
226-250				1	1	4		2		1	9
251-275							1				1
276-300						1	3	2			6
Totals	4	13	10	16	17	21	13	9	0	1	104

Figure 14.5: Correlation table of fiction and non-fiction issues by a library

Examples

Represent the following sets of data in appropriate tables and/or diagrams:

14.1 The number of book issues to students and to staff from a number of different departments of a university in the course of a year were as follows:

Department	Students	Staff
Agriculture	396	70
Anthropology	1122	340
Botany	562	181
Chemistry	737	473
Computing	557	233
Crystallography	149	33
Engineering	1044	434
Geology	1579	556
General science	311	273

Department	Students	Staff
Mathematics	710	437
Mineralogy	52	22
Physics	1446	704
Psychology	1153	495
Zoology	1343	462

14.2 The size of population and number of library loans for a random sample of major cities were as follows:

Population (100,000)	Number of loans (100,000)
114.5	86.0
25.9	35.8
4.2	51.3
7.5	47.3
6.7	7.5
6.5	94.7
6.0	77.0
5.9	39.9
4.6	18.0
4.5	36.0
4.3	68.9

14.3 The frequency of use of a number of documents of different ages is as follows:

Age of document (Years)	Frequency of use (Times/year)
1	40
3	18
2	30
4	21
3	26
5	10
4	13
3	35

14.4 Data relating to the stock and issues of twelve libraries are:

Live stock (thousands)	Daily issues
1.09	24
7.42	92

4.20	67
8.25	158
8.81	81
1.62	59
3.84	54
9.40	171
3.63	100
14.10	276
2.50	122
11.47	200

14.5 The following table gives the approximate number of abstracts (in thousands) in a selection of volumes of abstracts published in 1977, together with the cost of each volume:

No of abstracts (thousands)	Cost (£)
36.7	115
8.5	52
12.5	75
3.9	31
0.5	9
1.3	12
4.1	20
19.4	56
4.3	24

14.6 An analysis of interlending provided the following data of the numbers of items obtained and the number of items supplied by each of a selection of libraries in a period of twelve months:

Library	No of items obtained	No of items supplied
1	920	874
2	2174	489
3	468	1175
4	608	1134
5	276	1752
6	874	588
7	744	270
8	484	822

14.7 The cost (in £) and number of pages in the books noted in a publisher's list were:

Cost	Pages	Cost	Pages	Cost	Pages
19.95	496	27.50	392	21.00	240
9.95	208	12.50	200	15.00	278
17.50	300	25.00	280	27.50	420
15.00	448	8.00	120	10.50	128
12.00	200	5.95	220	9.95	249
30.00	288	9.95	200	35.00	392
32.50	324	32.50	468	20.00	400
35.00	525	24.00	539	27.50	300
37.50	384	30.00	400	15.00	240
25.00	250	30.00	320	16.00	230
18.00	200	35.00	736	12.00	144
15.00	224	22.00	516	45.00	336
30.00	384	45.00	700	40.00	550
25.00	256	20.00	400	30.00	478
17.50	215	30.00	656	17.50	437
17.00	278	9.50	191	9.95	288
20.00	376	19.50	464	18.50	496
22.50	421	20.50	348	18.00	236
32.50	450	30.00	352	12.00	143
30.00	243	32.50	598	17.00	284
12.00	202	27.50	392	28.00	520
15.00	251	24.00	472	55.00	758
21.00	320	55.00	591	25.00	413
35.00	460	14.50	282	27.50	394
12.00	342	21.00	340	17.00	207
35.00	440	7.50	88	21.00	351
25.00	292	37.50	464	24.00	344
12.50	130	22.50	382	25.00	402
20.00	249	18.00	182	45.00	458
3.50	63	30.00	400	21.50	278
27.50	508	16.00	256	30.00	368
15.00	275	12.50	112	40.00	458
7.50	83				

Chapter 15

CORRELATION

It was shown in Chapter 14 that when observations involve two quantitative variables, they can be represented in a scatter diagram. The association between the measured variables is known as *correlation*. Such data are tabulated in Figure 14.1 and presented graphically in the scatter diagram of Figure 14.2. Since the increasing cost of books is associated with an increasing number of pages, the correlation is said to be positive. This is characterized in the scatter diagram by the points being clustered around an imaginary straight line sloping upwards towards the right. If the points cluster close to the line, they are said to exhibit a strong correlation; if they are more widely scattered, the correlation is weak.

A different form of correlation will arise when relating the frequency of use of a document with its age. The greater the age of the document, the less frequently it may be used — as illustrated in Figure 15.1. In this case, the correlation is said to be negative and, in a scatter diagram, the points will cluster about an imaginary straight line sloping upwards towards the left (Figure 15.2).

Document	Age of document (years)	Frequency of use (times per year)
1	1	40
2	2	30
3	3	26
4	3	18
5	4	13
6	5	10
7	5	8

Figure 15.1: Data showing negative correlation

174

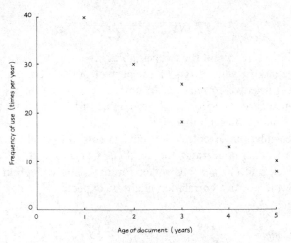

Figure 15.2: Negative correlation

If there is no correlation between the variables, the points in the scatter diagram are not clustered along an imaginary line but are dispersed in all directions as shown in Figure 15.3.

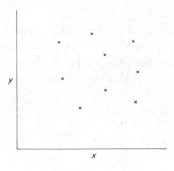

Figure 15.3: No correlation

Whilst the scatter diagram provides a useful qualitative picture of the correlation between two variables, a quantitative measure is often required. Such a measure is provided by the *correlation coefficient*. There are two coefficients commonly in use, the *Pearson correlation coefficient* and the *Spearman correlation coefficient*.

The Pearson correlation coefficient, applied to two variables which are distributed normally, is represented by *r* and is expressed as:

175

$$r = \frac{\Sigma XY - n\overline{X}\,\overline{Y}}{\sqrt{(\Sigma X^2 - n\overline{X}^2) \cdot (\Sigma Y^2 - n\overline{Y}^2)}}$$

where X and Y represent the two variables involved.

The value of r varies from $+1$ for perfect positive correlation to -1 for perfect negative correlation. In both cases, all the points would lie on the imaginary straight line. A zero value of r indicates that X and Y are independent of each other.

The calculation of correlation coefficients will be illustrated with reference to data concerning the number of entries made in (a) a Peek-a-boo index and (b) a KWIC index for the same collection of documents. Some positive correlation might be expected. The data are given in Figure 15.4.

Document number	1	2	3	4	5	6	7	8	9	10	11	12
No of entries in Peek-a-boo index	2	3	3	3	4	4	4	5	5	5	5	6
No of entries in KWIC index	5	3	5	6	4	5	6	2	3	5	7	6

Figure 15.4: Numbers of entries made for a set of documents in Peek-a-boo and KWIC indexes

If the two variables are represented by X and Y, letting X represent the number of entries in the Peek-a-boo index and Y represent the number of entries in the KWIC index, the data can be re-tabulated — together with further data calculated from them — in Figure 15.5.

From Figure 15.5:

$$\Sigma XY = 233$$
$$n = 12$$
$$\overline{X} = 4.08$$
$$\overline{Y} = 4.75$$
$$\Sigma X^2 = 215$$
$$\overline{X}^2 = 16.65$$
$$\Sigma Y^2 = 295$$
$$\overline{Y}^2 = 22.56$$

Hence:

176

Document	X	X²	Y	Y²	XY
1	2	4	5	25	10
2	3	9	3	9	9
3	3	9	5	25	15
4	3	9	6	36	18
5	4	16	4	16	16
6	4	16	5	25	20
7	4	16	6	36	24
8	5	25	2	4	10
9	5	25	3	9	15
10	5	25	5	25	25
11	5	25	7	49	35
12	6	36	6	36	36
Totals	49	215	57	295	233

Figure 15.5: Tabulated data relating to two variables X and Y for calculating r

$$r = \frac{233 - 12 \times 4.08 \times 4.75}{\sqrt{(215 - 12 \times 16.65) \cdot (295 - 12 \times 22.56)}}$$

$$= \frac{0.44}{\sqrt{15.20 \times 24.28}}$$

$$= \frac{0.44}{19.21}$$

$$= 0.023$$

This result suggests that there is virtually no correlation between the number of entries for a document in the KWIC index and the number of entries for the document in a Peek-a-boo index.

Since the above result was obtained from only a sample of the whole population of documents, there could be a discrepancy due to sampling between the result and the value of r that would be derived from observations on the whole population. The null hypothesis would be that there is no correlation between the two variables other than that due to chance and it is necessary to determine whether the calculated value of r is significantly different from zero. To do this, a t-test is performed, t being calculated from:

$$t = r\sqrt{\frac{n-2}{1-r^2}}$$

In the above example:

$$t = 0.023\sqrt{\frac{12-2}{1-0.023^2}}$$

$$= 0.073$$

In this type of t-test, the number of degrees of freedom is $(n-2)$. In the example, $(n-2)$ is equal to 10 and, for 10 degrees of freedom, the 0.05 and 0.01 significance levels, obtained from the table of t (Appendix 5) are 2.228 and 3.169 respectively.

Hence, it can be concluded that the calculated value of r is not significantly different from zero and therefore the number of entries in the KWIC index and in the Peek-a-boo index appear to be independent. Alternatively, there may be insufficient evidence to decide conclusively whether to accept or reject the null hypothesis — in which case the process may usefully be repeated on a larger sample. On the other hand, the correlation coefficient may appear to be quite high but a t-test may show it to be not significantly different from zero. This occurs if, yet again, too small a sample is taken. Whatever the size of the sample, r should be at least ± 0.4 before it can be said that any significant correlation exists but, as the sample size gets smaller, a correlation coefficient as high as 0.7 − 0.8 may be necessary to signify good correlation between two variables.

Even so, a significant result should be treated with some caution since the apparent correlation may be due to coincidence or to independent relationships between the observed variables and some other factor or factors. For example, frequent use of the library by students may be associated with high examination marks yet the visits to the library may be simply to read the daily newspaper and the high examination marks may be due to diligent attendance at lectures!

In some cases, the magnitudes of the variables may be large, making the computation of r particularly tedious. In other cases, the actual magnitudes of the variables may not be known. For example, a group of boys and a group of girls may put their favourite authors in order of preference and the purpose of the investigation would be to determine whether there is any correlation between the choice of the two sexes.

In these circumstances, the Spearman correlation coefficient is

178

calculated. Using the data from Figure 15.5 in order to illustrate the method, the X and Y values are tabulated in the second and third columns of Figure 15.6.

Although the values of the X variable are here shown in an array, there is no need to spend time putting the data in such order — the raw data can be listed in the order in which they are collected.

Document	X	Y	Ranked X	Ranked Y	D (Ranked X minus Ranked Y)	D^2
1	2	5	1	$6\frac{1}{2}$	$-5\frac{1}{2}$	$30\frac{1}{4}$
2	3	3	3	$2\frac{1}{2}$	$\frac{1}{2}$	$\frac{1}{4}$
3	3	5	3	$6\frac{1}{2}$	$-3\frac{1}{2}$	$12\frac{1}{4}$
4	3	6	3	10	-7	49
5	4	4	6	4	2	4
6	4	5	6	$6\frac{1}{2}$	$-\frac{1}{2}$	$\frac{1}{4}$
7	4	6	6	10	-4	16
8	5	2	$9\frac{1}{2}$	1	$8\frac{1}{2}$	$72\frac{1}{4}$
9	5	3	$9\frac{1}{2}$	$2\frac{1}{2}$	7	49
10	5	5	$9\frac{1}{2}$	$6\frac{1}{2}$	3	9
11	5	7	$9\frac{1}{2}$	12	$-2\frac{1}{2}$	$6\frac{1}{4}$
12	6	6	12	10	2	4
Total						$252\frac{1}{2}$

Figure 15.6: Tabulated data relating to two variables X and Y for calculating ρ

The fourth and fifth columns show the ranked order of the X and Y values. The lowest value of the variable is labelled as 'rank 1', the next lowest as 'rank 2' and so on until each value of the variable has been given a rank number. In this example, the highest value of the variable is ranked 12. If several observations have the same magnitudes of the variable, they are all given the same rank number, being the average of the observation numbers involved. Thus, as the value of X is 5 for the 8th, 9th, 10th and 11th observations, they are all ranked:

$$\frac{8 + 9 + 10 + 11}{4}$$

ie $9\frac{1}{2}$

The Spearman rank order coefficient is represented by ρ and is calculated from the expression:

$$\rho = 1 - \frac{6\Sigma D^2}{n(n^2 - 1)}$$

where D is the difference between the ranked value of X and the ranked value of Y.

The Spearman coefficient ranges from +1 for perfect positive correlation to -1 for perfect negative correlation.

From Figure 15.6,

$$\Sigma D^2 = 252\tfrac{1}{2}$$
$$n = 12$$

Hence:

$$\rho = 1 - \frac{6 \times 252\tfrac{1}{2}}{12 \times 143}$$

$$= 0.12$$

If there is any correlation between X and Y, it would appear to be weak, but the significance of the result can be assessed in the same way as the significance of r.

Thus:

$$t = \rho \sqrt{\frac{n - 2}{1 - \rho^2}}$$

In the above example:

$$t = 0.12 \sqrt{\frac{12 - 2}{1 - 0.12^2}}$$

$$= 0.38$$

This is again appreciably less than the values of t for the 5% and 1% significance levels and 10 degrees of freedom, and so the conclusion must be either that X and Y are independent or the sample is too small to give any evidence to the contrary.

Whilst the Spearman coefficient is simpler to calculate than the Pearson coefficient, it must be appreciated that the actual values of X and Y are not involved and therefore the value of ρ is less reliable than the value of r.

To take another example, the number of abstracts in the 1971, 1972 and 1973 issues of *Lead abstracts* were counted. Since the abstracts are of varying length, the number of pages taken up is not in direct proportion to the number of abstracts. However, some strong positive correlation might be expected. The data for calculating the Pearson correlation coefficient are given in Figure 15.7.

Date	Number of pages (X)	Number of abstracts (Y)	X^2	Y^2	XY
Jan 71	61	15	3721	225	915
Mar 71	118	28	13924	784	3304
May 71	57	15	3249	225	855
Jul 71	123	30	15129	900	3690
Sep 71	125	31	15625	961	3875
Nov 71	122	30	14884	900	3660
Jan 72	122	30	14884	900	3660
Mar 72	85	23	7225	529	1955
May 72	85	22	7225	484	1870
Jul 72	85	22	7225	484	1870
Sep 72	83	23	6889	529	1909
Nov 72	78	23	6084	529	1794
Jan 73	76	23	5776	529	1748
Mar 73	76	21	5776	441	1596
May 73	73	21	5329	441	1533
Jul 73	70	21	4900	441	1470
Sep 73	97	25	9409	625	2425
Nov 73	107	29	11449	841	3103
Totals	1643	432	158703	10768	41232

*Figure 15.7: Tabulated data relating to numbers of abstracts and pages in **Lead abstracts** for calculating r*

From Figure 15.7:

$$\Sigma XY = 41232$$
$$n = 18$$
$$\bar{X} = 91.3$$
$$\bar{Y} = 24.0$$
$$\Sigma X^2 = 158703$$

181

$$\bar{X}^2 = 8335.7$$
$$\Sigma Y^2 = 10768$$
$$\bar{Y}^2 = 576$$

Hence:

$$r = \frac{41232 - 18 \times 91.3 \times 24.0}{\sqrt{(158703 - 18 \times 8335.7) \cdot (10768 - 18 \times 576)}}$$

$$= \frac{1790.4}{\sqrt{8660.4 \times 400}}$$

$$= 0.96$$

This result suggests that there is a very strong correlation between the number of abstracts and the number of pages in issues of *Lead abstracts*. A *t*-test can be performed, as previously explained, to confirm the result. Thus:

$$t = r\sqrt{\frac{n-2}{1-r^2}}$$

$$= 0.96\sqrt{\frac{18-2}{1-0.96^2}}$$

$$= 13.7$$

Since the number of degrees of freedom is 16, the 0.05 and 0.01 significance values, obtained from the table of *t*, are 2.120 and 2.921 respectively, confirming the strong correlation between number of abstracts and number of pages.

Using the same data, the Spearman correlation coefficient can be calculated as already described. The necessary data are tabulated in Figure 15.8.

From Figure 15.8:

$$\Sigma D^2 = 56\tfrac{1}{2}$$
$$n = 18$$

Hence:

$$\rho = 1 - \frac{6 \times 56\tfrac{1}{2}}{18(18^2-1)}$$

$$= 0.942$$

182

Date	Number of pages (X)	Number of abstracts (Y)	Ranked X	Ranked Y	D	D^2
Jan 71	61	15	2	$1\frac{1}{2}$	$\frac{1}{2}$	$\frac{1}{4}$
Mar 71	118	28	14	13	1	1
May 71	57	15	1	$1\frac{1}{2}$	$-\frac{1}{2}$	$\frac{1}{4}$
Jul 71	123	30	17	16	1	1
Sep 71	125	31	18	18	0	0
Nov 71	122	30	$15\frac{1}{2}$	16	$-\frac{1}{2}$	$\frac{1}{4}$
Jan 72	122	30	$15\frac{1}{2}$	16	$-\frac{1}{2}$	$\frac{1}{4}$
Mar 72	85	23	10	$9\frac{1}{2}$	$\frac{1}{2}$	$\frac{1}{4}$
May 72	85	22	10	$6\frac{1}{2}$	$3\frac{1}{2}$	$12\frac{1}{4}$
Jul 72	85	22	10	$6\frac{1}{2}$	$3\frac{1}{2}$	$12\frac{1}{4}$
Sep 72	83	23	8	$9\frac{1}{2}$	$-1\frac{1}{2}$	$2\frac{1}{4}$
Nov 72	78	23	7	$9\frac{1}{2}$	$-2\frac{1}{2}$	$6\frac{1}{4}$
Jan 73	76	23	$5\frac{1}{2}$	$9\frac{1}{2}$	-4	16
Mar 73	76	21	$5\frac{1}{2}$	4	$1\frac{1}{2}$	$2\frac{1}{4}$
May 73	73	21	4	4	0	0
Jul 73	70	21	3	4	-1	1
Sep 73	97	25	12	12	0	0
Nov 73	107	29	13	14	-1	1
Total						$56\frac{1}{2}$

Figure 15.8: Tabulated data relating to numbers of abstracts and pages in Lead abstracts for calculating ρ

Once again, a strong positive correlation between the number of abstracts and the number of pages per issue is shown.

If the data are grouped — as in Figure 14.5 — the X and Y values are taken as the mid-points of the groups. The data of Figure 14.5 are re-tabulated in Figure 15.9 to show the mid-point values. If the number of non-fiction issues is taken as the X variable, there is a total of 4 observations of 3 non-fiction issues, a total of 13 observations of 8 non-fiction issues, and so on.

Hence:

$$\Sigma X = (3 \times 4) + (8 \times 13) + (13 \times 10) + (18 \times 16) \ldots + (48 \times 1)$$

$$= 2332$$

Similarly, if Y is taken as the number of fiction issues:

183

	Grouped data data	Mid-point	

<table>
<tr><td colspan="3"></td><td colspan="11" align="center">*Number of non-fiction issues*</td></tr>
</table>

Grouped data data	Mid-point	1-5	6-10	11-15	16-20	21-25	26-30	31-35	36-40	41-45	46-50	Totals
		3	8	13	18	23	28	33	38	43	48	
26-50	38	1	4									5
51-75	63	3	5	3								11
76-100	88		3	1	1							5
101-125	113		1	4	3	4	1	1				14
126-150	138				5	6	1	1				13
151-175	163			2	4	3	6	2	1			18
176-200	188				1	2	5	2	1			11
201-225	213				1	1	3	3	3			11
226-250	238				1		4	1	2		1	9
251-275	263						1					1
276-300	288					1		3	2			6
Totals		4	13	10	16	17	21	13	9	0	1	104

Number of fiction issues (row label at left of fiction ranges)

Figure 15.9: Correlation table of fiction and non-fiction issues showing mid-points of groups

$$\Sigma Y = (38 \times 5) + (63 \times 11) + (88 \times 5) \ldots + (288 \times 6)$$

$$= 16177$$

$$\Sigma XY = (3 \times 38 \times 1) + (8 \times 38 \times 4) + (3 \times 63 \times 3) \ldots$$

$$\ldots + (38 \times 288 \times 2)$$

$$= 415916$$

$$\Sigma X^2 = (3^2 \times 4) + (8^2 \times 13) + (13^2 \times 10) \ldots + (48^2 \times 1)$$

$$= 62656$$

$$\Sigma Y^2 = (38^2 \times 5) + (63^2 \times 11) + (88^2 \times 5) \ldots + (288^2 \times 6)$$

$$= 2958651$$

$$n = 104$$

Hence:

$$r = \frac{415916 - 104 \times \dfrac{2332}{104} \times \dfrac{16177}{104}}{\sqrt{\left(62656 - 104 \times \dfrac{2332^2}{104^2}\right) \cdot \left(2958651 - 104 \times \dfrac{16177^2}{104^2}\right)}}$$

$$= 0.785$$

Whilst a value of r has been obtained, the numbers involved were large to handle. This situation can be avoided by adjusting the scales of X and Y.

As far as the X variable is concerned, one of the mid-point values near the centre is taken to be zero and the mid-point values to the left are replaced by -1, -2, -3 etc whilst the mid-point values to the right are replaced by $+1$, $+2$, $+3$ etc.

Hence, instead of the scale being:

| 3 | 8 | 13 | 18 | 23 | 28 | 33 | 38 | 43 | 48 |

it becomes:

| -4 | -3 | -2 | -1 | 0 | $+1$ | $+2$ | $+3$ | $+4$ | $+5$ |

Similarly, instead of the Y scale being:

| 38 | 63 | 88 | 113 | 138 | 163 | 188 | 213 | 238 | 263 | 288 |

it becomes:

| -5 | -4 | -3 | -2 | -1 | 0 | $+1$ | $+2$ | $+3$ | $+4$ | $+5$ |

And the table of Figure 15.9 is modified to that of Figure 15.10. Now:

$$\Sigma X = (-4 \times 4) + (-3 \times 13) + (-2 \times 10) \ldots + (+5 \times 1)$$
$$= -12$$

$$\Sigma Y = (-5 \times 5) + (-4 \times 11) + (-3 \times 5) \ldots + (+5 \times 6)$$
$$= -31$$

$$\Sigma XY = (-4 \times -5 \times 1) + (-3 \times -5 \times 4) \ldots + (+3 \times +5 \times 2)$$
$$= 429$$

	Number of non-fiction issues										
	−4	−3	−2	−1	0	+1	+2	+3	+4	+5	Totals
−5	1	4									5
−4	3	5	3								11
−3		3	1	1							5
−2		1	4	3	4	1	1				14
−1				5	6	1	1				13
0			2	4	3	6	2	1			18
+1				1	2	5	2	1			11
+2					1	1	3	3	3		11
+3					1		4	1	2	1	9
+4						1					1
+5						1		3	2		6
Totals	4	13	10	16	17	21	13	9	0	1	104

(Number of fiction issues — row labels at left)

Figure 15.10: Correlation table of fiction and non-fiction issues with simplified scales

$$\Sigma X^2 = ((-4)^2 \times 4) + ((-3)^2 \times 13) \ldots + ((+5)^2 \times 1)$$

$$= 416$$

$$\Sigma Y^2 = ((-5)^2 \times 5) + ((-4)^2 \times 11) \ldots + ((+5)^2 \times 6)$$

$$= 717$$

$$n = 104$$

Hence:

$$r = \frac{429 - 104 \times \frac{-12}{104} \times \frac{-31}{104}}{\sqrt{\left(416 - 104 \times \frac{(-12)^2}{104^2}\right) \cdot \left(717 - 104 \times \frac{(-31)^2}{104^2}\right)}}$$

$$= 0.785 \text{ as before}$$

Whilst care must be taken over the negative quantities, it will be apparent that the numbers involved are much simpler.

Examples
Determine correlation coefficients for the data in Examples 14.1 to 14.7.

Chapter 16

REGRESSION

In defining correlation in Chapter 15, mention was made of an imaginary straight line about which the points in the scatter diagram cluster when positive or negative correlation is present. However, it would be much more useful if, instead of imagining a straight line, a definite line could be described which is most representative of the observations clustered about it.

As shown in Figure 16.1, a variety of straight lines might reasonably be drawn through a collection of points in a scatter diagram but a 'best' straight line can be determined mathematically by a procedure known as the 'method of least squares'. This best straight line is known as the *regression line*.

Any straight line can be represented by an equation:

$$y = a + bx$$

In Figure 16.2, x and y represent the values of the X and Y variables respectively at any point on the line, whilst, for a particular line,

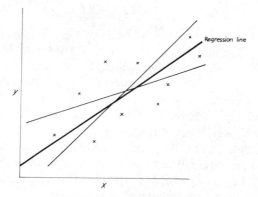

Figure 16.1: Straight lines drawn through a set of points

a and *b* are constant. The constant *a* is the intercept of the line on the *Y* axis and *b* is the slope of the line (ie it rises by a distance *b* in the *Y* direction in unit distance in the *X* direction). Hence, if the values of *a* and *b* can be determined, it is possible to determine from the equation for the line that value of *y* which corresponds to a given value of *x*.

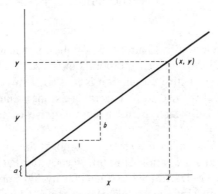

Figure 16.2: Parameters of a straight line

By applying the method of least squares, it can be found that:

$$a = \bar{Y} - b\bar{X}$$

and:

$$b = \frac{\Sigma XY - n\bar{X}\bar{Y}}{\Sigma X^2 - n\bar{X}^2}$$

Given the *X* and *Y* values of a set of observations, the values of *a* and *b* can be calculated and inserted in the equation $y = a + bx$. This is then the equation of the line known as the *regression line of y on x*, and *b* is known as the *regression coefficient of y on x*.

Hence, if any value of the *X* variable is given, the corresponding value of the *Y* variable can be calculated.

For example, given the data concerning the number of pages occupied by abstracts tabulated in Figure 15.7, if the number of pages is specified, the equation for the regression line will enable the number of abstracts that could be printed to be estimated.

Thus:

188

$$\Sigma XY = 41232$$
$$n = 18$$
$$\bar{X} = 91.3$$
$$\bar{Y} = 24.0$$
$$\Sigma X^2 = 158703$$
$$\bar{X}^2 = 8335.7$$

Hence:

$$b = \frac{41232 - 18 \times 91.3 \times 24.0}{158703 - 18 \times 8335.7}$$

$$= \frac{41232 - 39441.6}{158703 - 150042.6}$$

$$= \frac{1790.4}{8660.4}$$

$$= 0.21$$

and:

$$a = 24.0 - 0.21 \times 91.3$$

$$= 4.83$$

Thus, the regression line of y on x is given by the equation:

$$y = 4.83 + 0.21x$$

By using this equation, it is easily calculated that the number of abstracts which one could expect to print on (say) 100 pages would be 4.83 + 21, ie 25.83.

Conversely, it may be required to know how many pages would be required to accommodate a given number of abstracts which involves determining the *regression line of x on y*. This is not the same line as the regression line of y on x and has the equation:

$$x = a^* + b^*y$$

Note that the constants in this equation are different from those in the regression line of y on x and therefore have been distinguished by the superscripts. However, they are found from similar expressions, viz:

$$a^* = \bar{X} - b^*\bar{Y}$$

and

$$b^* = \frac{\Sigma XY - n\overline{X}\,\overline{Y}}{\Sigma Y^2 - n\overline{Y}^2}$$

Now, if values of a^* and b^* are entered in the equation, if any value of the Y variable is specified, the corresponding value of the X variable can be calculated. So, using the data from Figure 15.7:

$$b^* = \frac{41232 - 18 \times 91.3 \times 24.0}{10768 - 18 \times 576}$$

$$= \frac{41232 - 39441.6}{10768 - 10368}$$

$$= \frac{1790.4}{400}$$

$$= 4.48$$

$$a^* = 91.3 - 4.48 \times 24.0$$

$$= -16.22$$

Thus, the regression line is:

$$x = 4.48y - 16.22$$

From this equation, it can be deduced that (say) 30 abstracts may be expected to occupy ($4.48 \times 30 - 16.22$), ie 118.18 pages of *Lead abstracts*.

The need for the two regression lines to be different can be seen if we consider, for the sake of argument, that 100 pages contain 25 abstracts. If it were desired to estimate how many abstracts could be contained on 100 pages, it would be best to estimate on the low side, ie rather less than 25 in order to ensure that there is sufficient space available. On the other hand, if it were desired to estimate the space needed to accommodate 25 abstracts, it would be best to estimate on the high side, ie rather more than 100 pages in order again to ensure that there would be sufficient space available.

In the first example, we cannot be certain that 100 pages would contain exactly 25.83 abstracts. There is a degree of uncertainty that can be specified by determining 95% confidence limits. The standard deviation of the observations from the regression line of y on x — sometimes referred to as the *standard error about the line* — is given by:

$$\sqrt{\frac{\Sigma Y^2 - n\bar{Y}^2}{n-1}} \times \sqrt{1-r^2}$$

where r is the Pearson correlation coefficient.

Using the data for the above example, the standard error in the Y direction will be:

$$\sqrt{\frac{10768 - 18 \times 576}{17}} \times \sqrt{1 - 0.96^2}$$

$$= \sqrt{23.53} \times \sqrt{0.0784}$$

$$= \sqrt{1.845}$$

$$= 1.36$$

Since 95% of all observations fall within two standard deviations of the mean, in this example 95% of the observations should lie between the two lines parallel to the line of regression and spaced from it by a distance of 2×1.36, ie 2.72 parallel to the Y axis. The observations, line of regression of y on x, and the limits within which 95% of the observations fall are shown in Figure 16.3.

Hence, 100 pages can be said, with 95% certainty to contain between $(25.83 - 2.72)$ and $(25.83 + 2.72)$ abstracts, ie between approximately 23 and $28\frac{1}{2}$.

If the regression line of x on y is being used, the standard error about the line is given by:

$$\sqrt{\frac{\Sigma X^2 - n\bar{X}^2}{n-1}} \times \sqrt{1-r^2}$$

Again using the data from the above example, the standard error in the X direction will be:

$$\sqrt{\frac{158703 - 18 \times 8335.7}{17}} \times \sqrt{1 - 0.96^2}$$

$$= \sqrt{509.44} \times \sqrt{0.0784}$$

$$= \sqrt{39.94}$$

$$= 6.32$$

Hence, 30 abstracts can be said, with 95% certainty to occupy between $(118.18 - 2 \times 6.32)$ and $(118.18 + 2 \times 6.32)$ pages, ie between approximately $105\frac{1}{2}$ and 131.

It will be appreciated that a more precise estimate would be obtained by taking a larger sample.

191

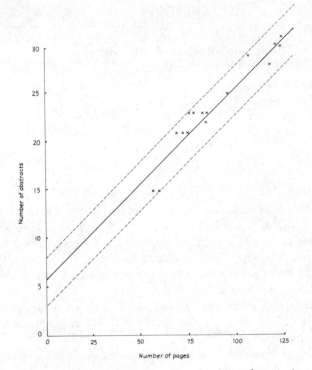

*Figure 16.3: Scatter diagram showing line of regression
of y on x and 95% limits*

Examples

16.1 From the data of Example 14.1, estimate the number of issues that may be expected for students if there were 400 issues to the staff of a department.

16.2 From the data of Example 14.2, estimate the number of loans that would be expected for a population of 1,000,000.

16.3 From the data of Example 14.3, estimate how old a document is likely to be before there is no demand for it.

16.4 From the data of Example 14.4, estimate the number of daily issues that might be expected from a live stock of 5000 items.

16.5 From the data of Example 14.5, estimate (a) the number of abstracts you would expect in a volume costing £40 and (b) the cost of a volume containing 10,000 abstracts.

192

16.6 From the data of Example 14.6, estimate (a) the number of items that might be supplied by a library that borrows 1000 items and (b) the number of items that a library might borrow if it supplies 1000 items.

Part V

MECHANIZATION

Chapter 17

COMPUTER PACKAGES

Statistical calculations can be lengthy procedures, especially when large quantities of data are involved and large samples are taken in order to increase precision. To aid calculation, various computer programs have been written, a prominent one of which is the Statistical Package for the Social Sciences — usually referred to as SPSS.

SPSS can perform a very wide range of statistical operations which are described in detail by Nie et al. In this introductory text, only a few will be described to illustrate some of the applications of such packages.

To investigate problems relating to book issues, two main sets of data are required, viz the raw data to be analysed and the program of instructions to the computer that enables it to analyse the raw data as required.

In collecting data on book issues, the month and day of the week on which each observation was made were recorded, together with the numbers of issues of adult fiction and non-fiction and junior fiction and non-fiction.

The purposes of an investigation may be to derive information about the number of issues of a specific category of book, possibly on specified days and/or in specified months. Any correlation between the numbers of issues of two categories of book may also be of interest.

The data can be input to the computer via punched cards, as also can the controlling program. The whole procedure involves a number of steps as outlined below.

1   Decide on the coding of each variable. The days of the week can be numbered from 1 to 6, corresponding to Monday to Saturday respectively. One column on the punched card will be required to code that information.

The months of the year can be coded similarly but, since there are twelve months, two columns will be required to accommodate numbers 01 to 12.

The numbers of adult fiction and adult non-fiction issues could exceed 1000 per day and therefore each of these variables requires an allocation of four columns. On the other hand, junior issues do not exceed 999 and therefore three columns are sufficient for junior fiction and another three columns for junior non-fiction.

It is also desirable to identify each record and since the data included observations for 234 days, three columns are required to specify any number from 001 to 234.

From that analysis, it will be apparent that a total of twenty columns is needed to record the data for each observation. It is helpful to punch operators if the data to be punched are kept in discrete groups of not more than about six or seven columns, rather than a single block of figures. Therefore, with that in mind, the columns on the card to be used for each variable can be specified.

A list of the data can now be compiled, showing a coded name for each variable (eg JUFIC for 'junior fiction') and the columns in which the data are to be recorded. In addition, the data list should include the *variable labels* to make clear the meanings of the variable names, and the *value labels* to indicate the meanings of the codes used. The table is shown in Figure 17.1.

There is no necessity to specify value labels for FICTION, NONFIC, JUFIC, JUNOFIC and PERSON since the data recorded on the punched card are the actual number of issues etc, not a coded representation as is the case with DAY and MONTH.

2 In accordance with the decisions recorded in the data list table, the data for each record are entered in the appropriate columns of a punching instruction form. Even though, for some reason, data are missing, something should be recorded in the columns of the card in which the computer will be instructed to expect to find data. Therefore, codes for missing values for each variable must be specified. These codes are values which would not otherwise occur. Therefore 9 can be used to indicate that the day in question has not been recorded, 99 to indicate that the month has not been recorded, 999 that the junior fiction and junior non-fiction values are missing, and 9999 that the adult fiction and non-fiction values are missing. Figure 17.2 shows the punching instructions required to create a file (which was called STATS) and enter the data for the first twelve observations made.

3 In order to run a program, a set of control cards is required to provide the computer with the essential information it needs to manipulate the data in the file.

198

Variable name	Variable label	Column(s)	Value label
DAY	Day of week	1	1 Monday
			2 Tuesday
			3 Wednesday
			4 Thursday
			5 Friday
			6 Saturday
			9 No data
MONTH	Month	6-7	01 January
			02 February
			03 March
			04 April
			05 May
			06 June
			07 July
			08 August
			09 September
			10 October
			11 November
			12 December
			99 No data
FICTION	Number of fiction issues	11-14	9999 No data
NONFIC	Number of non-fiction issues	21-24	9999 No data
JUFIC	Number of junior fiction issues	31-33	999 No data
JUNOFIC	Number of junior non-fiction issues	41-43	999 No data
PERSON	Identification number	78-80	

Figure 17.1: Data list table

The commands consist of a 'control field' punched in columns 1-15 and a 'specification field' punched in columns 16-80. The complete listing of a program run on an IBM 370/168 computer, shown in Figure 17.3, is preceded only by a sign-on card, a password, and an instruction to run the program, thus:

$SIG userid T=? P=?
password
$RUN *SPSS 8=STATS 6=*SINK*@MCC

Col 1			
$SIG Sheild
password
$CREATE STATS
$COPY * SOURCE * STATS

	6–7	8–11	21–24	31–33	41–43	77–80
1	04	1542	1307	089	040	001
2	04	1565	1253	106	045	002
3	04	1405	1220	076	031	003
4	04	1475	1523	104	020	004
5	04	1275	1064	093	006	005
6	04	1246	1239	234	080	006
1	04	1716	1317	077	040	007
2	04	1826	1258	108	035	008
3	04	1933	1215	088	023	009
4	04	2051	1596	145	056	010
5	04	9999	9999	999	999	011
6	04	9999	9999	999	999	012

$ENDFILE

$SIG

Figure 17.2: Punching instructions for creating a file of data on book issues

The first of these cards includes the appropriate user identifier and global figures for the central processing unit time and number of pages of printout required. The second card signifies the user's password and the Run card shows that unit 8 of the disk file contains the raw data that was put into the file called STATS ready for input to SPSS. The output of SPSS is to be put into unit 6, using Machine Carriage Control as a paper-saving device.

```
 1 RUN NAME        LIBRARY ISSUE STATISTICS
 2 PAGESIZE        NOEJECT
 3 DATA LIST       FIXED(1)/1 DAY 1  MONTH 6-7  FICTION 11-14  NONFIC 21-24
 4                 JUFIC 31-33  JUNOFIC 41-43  PERSON 78-80
 5 INPUT MEDIUM    DISK
 6 N OF CASES      20
 7 VAR LABELS      DAY,DAY OF WEEK/
 8                 MONTH,MONTH/
 9                 FICTION,NO OF FICTION ISSUES/
10                 NONFIC,NO OF NON-FICTION ISSUES/
11                 JUFIC,NO OF JUNIOR FICTION ISSUES/
12                 JUNOFIC,NO OF JUNIOR NON-FICTION ISSUES/
13                 PERSON,IDENTIFYING RESPONSE NUMBER/
14 VALUE LABELS    DAY (1) MONDAY  (2) TUESDAY  (3) WEDNESDAY  (4) THURSDAY
15                 (5) FRIDAY  (6) SATURDAY  (9) NO DATA/
16                 MONTH (01) JAN  (02) FEB  (03) MAR  (04) APR  (05) MAY  (06) JUN
17                 (07) JUL  (08) AUG  (09) SEP  (10) OCT  (11) NOV  (12) DEC
18                 (99) NO DATA/
19 MISSING VALUES  DAY(9)/MONTH(99)/JUFIC,JUNOFIC(999)/FICTION,NONFIC(9999)
20 FREQUENCIES     GENERAL=FICTION
21 READ INPUT DATA
```

Figure 17.3: SPSS program for library issue statistics

Explanations of the items in the listing of Figure 17.3 are:

Line 1 a heading to show the subject matter of the printout

Line 2 NOEJECT is another device to conserve paper by eliminating blank spaces between tabulations

Line 3 'Fixed' indicates that each card of input data has the same format. (1)/1 indicates that there is only one card per record and that first (and only) card contains the data specified. (If an investigation involved a large number of variables, more than one card per record may be required and that would have to be specified at this point.)

Line 5 The data are input from a disk store. If they are not previously recorded on disk and are to be entered from punched cards, then the computer would be so instructed at this point.

Line 6 The number of cases is specified.

Lines 7-13 A list of the variable names and labels. Note that each one is terminated by an oblique.

201

Lines 14-18 A list of value labels, again terminated by obliques.

Line 19 A list of the missing values, ie the codes to indicate when values of a variable have not been recorded.

Line 20 A command to print out the frequencies of occurrence for the specified variable name(s). 'General' signifies that the codes may be either numerical or alphabetical but, if alphabetical codes are used, various modifications to procedures are required that are not dealt with in this text. If frequencies for several variables are required, the form of statement would be:

GENERAL=FICTION, NONFIC

or GENERAL=FICTION TO JUNOFIC

or GENERAL=ALL

Line 21 An instruction to read the input data from the file.

4 The printout obtained as a result of running the program is shown in Figure 17.4.

```
FICTION   NO OF FICTION ISSUES
                                    RELATIVE   ADJUSTED    CUM
                            ABSOLUTE   FREQ       FREQ      FREQ
CATEGORY LABEL        CODE     FREQ    (PCT)      (PCT)     (PCT)
                      1205.      1      5.0        5.9       5.9
                      1246.      1      5.0        5.9      11.8
                      1275.      1      5.0        5.9      17.6
                      1405.      1      5.0        5.9      23.5
                      1439.      1      5.0        5.9      29.4
                      1474.      1      5.0        5.9      35.3
                      1542.      1      5.0        5.9      41.2
                      1565.      1      5.0        5.9      47.1
                      1607.      1      5.0        5.9      52.9
                      1682.      1      5.0        5.9      58.8
                      1713.      1      5.0        5.9      64.7
                      1716.      1      5.0        5.9      70.6
                      1826.      1      5.0        5.9      76.5
                      1837.      1      5.0        5.9      82.4
                      1933.      1      5.0        5.9      88.2
                      2030.      1      5.0        5.9      94.1
                      2051.      1      5.0        5.9     100.0
                      9999.      3     15.0      MISSING   100.0
                              ------   ------    ------
                      TOTAL     20    100.0     100.0

VALID CASES    17    MISSING CASES    3
```

Figure 17.4: Frequency table of fiction issues

Note the variable label printed at the top of the table.

The column headed **CODE** gives the actual numbers of fiction issues per day.

The column headed **ABSOLUTE FREQUENCY** gives the number of times the specified number of issues was observed.

The column headed **RELATIVE FREQUENCY** gives the number of times the specified number of issues was observed — as a percentage

202

of all observations.

The column headed **ADJUSTED FREQUENCY** gives the number of times the specified number of issues was observed – as a percentage of all valid observations (ie excluding the missing ones).

The column headed **CUMULATIVE FREQUENCY** gives the cumulative number of observations – as a percentage of all the valid observations.

It will be noted that, with this set of data, the result is an array with only a single observation of each value of the variable. This is obviously a situation in which the data should be grouped if a large number of observations is made. Figure 17.5 shows a modified listing in which JUFIC has been re-coded to form groups, each 25 issues in width. The printout for 234 cases is shown in Figure 17.6.

```
 1 RUN NAME          LIBRARY ISSUE STATISTICS
 2 PAGESIZE          NOEJECT
 3 DATA LIST         FIXED(1)/1 DAY 1  MONTH 6-7  FICTION 11-14  NONFIC 21-24
 4                   JUFIC 31-33  JUNOFIC 41-43  PERSON 78-80
 5 INPUT MEDIUM      DISK
 6 N OF CASES        234
 7 RECODE            JUFIC (001 THRU 025=01) (026 THRU 050=02) (051 THRU 075=03)
 8                   (076 THRU 100=04) (101 THRU 125=05) (126 THRU 150=06)
 9                   (151 THRU 175=07) (176 THRU 200=08) (201 THRU 225=09)
10                   (226 THRU 250=10) (251 THRU 275=11) (276 THRU 300=12)
11                   (999=99)
12 VAR LABELS        DAY,DAY OF WEEK/
13                   MONTH,MONTH/
14                   FICTION,NO OF FICTION ISSUES/
15                   NONFIC,NO OF NON-FICTION ISSUES/
16                   JUFIC,GROUPED JUNIOR FICTION ISSUES/
17                   JUNOFIC,NO OF JUNIOR NON-FICTION ISSUES/
18                   PERSON,IDENTIFYING RESPONSE NUMBER/
19 VALUE LABELS      DAY (1) MONDAY (2) TUESDAY (3) WEDNESDAY (4) THURSDAY
20                   (5) FRIDAY (6) SATURDAY (9) NO DATA/
21                   MONTH (01) JAN (02) FEB (03) MAR (04) APR (05) MAY (06) JUN
22                   (07) JUL (08) AUG (09) SEP (10) OCT (11) NOV (12) DEC
23                   (99) NO DATA/
24                   JUFIC (01) 001-025 (02) 026-050 (03) 051-075 (04) 076-100
25                   (05) 101-125 (06) 126-150 (07) 151-175 (08) 176-200
26                   (09) 201-225 (10) 226-250 (11) 251-275 (12) 276-300
27                   (99) NO DATA/
28 MISSING VALUES    DAY(9)/MONTH,JUFIC(99)/JUNOFIC(999)/FICTION,NONFIC(9999)
29 FREQUENCIES       GENERAL=JUFIC
30 OPTIONS           8
31 STATISTICS        1,3,4,5,8,9,10,11
32 READ INPUT DATA
```

Figure 17.5: SPSS program including a re-coding of junior fiction issues

5   A procedure (such as FREQUENCIES) can be followed by an OPTIONS card. The options available depend on the procedure involved but, as seen in Figure 17.5, Option 8 relating to FREQUENCIES has been specified in order to obtain the histogram of the JUFIC data shown in Figure 17.7.

6   Following an Options card (if any), a STATISTICS card may be inserted. Again, the available statistics will depend on the procedure

```
JUFIC     GROUPED JUNIOR FICTION ISSUES
                                      RELATIVE   ADJUSTED      CUM
                           ABSOLUTE     FREQ       FREQ       FREQ
CATEGORY LABEL      CODE     FREQ       (PCT)      (PCT)      (PCT)
026-050             2.        16         6.8        7.2        7.2
051-075             3.        56        23.9       25.3       32.6
076-100             4.        46        19.7       20.8       53.4
101-125             5.        40        17.1       18.1       71.5
126-150             6.        23         9.8       10.4       81.9
151-175             7.        11         4.7        5.0       86.9
176-200             8.        11         4.7        5.0       91.9
201-225             9.         9         3.8        4.1       95.9
226-250            10.         6         2.6        2.7       98.6
251-275            11.         3         1.3        1.4      100.0
NO DATA            99.        13         5.6      MISSING    100.0
                           ------     ------     ------
                 TOTAL      234        100.0      100.0
```

Figure 17.6: Grouped frequency table of junior fiction issues

```
JUFIC     GROUPED JUNIOR FICTION ISSUES
   CODE
       I
    2. I ********* (     16)
       I 026-050
       I
       I
    3. I ***************************** (     56)
       I 051-075
       I
       I
    4. I ************************* (     46)
       I 076-100
       I
       I
    5. I ********************* (     40)
       I 101-125
       I
       I
    6. I ************* (     23)
       I 126-150
       I
       I
    7. I ******* (     11)
       I 151-175
       I
       I
    8. I ******* (     11)
       I 176-200
       I
       I
    9. I ****** (      9)
       I 201-225
       I
       I
   10. I **** (      6)
       I 226-250
       I
       I
   11. I *** (      3)
       I 251-275
       I
       I
   99. I ******** (     13)
(MISSING) I NO DATA
       I
       I.........I.........I.........I.........I.........I
       0        20        40        60        80       100
       FREQUENCY
```

Figure 17.7: Histogram of grouped junior fiction issues

involved but, as seen in Figure 17.5, a number of statistics relating to FREQUENCIES have been specified, viz 1 — Mean, 3 — Median, 4 — Mode, 5 — Standard deviation, 8 — Skewness, 9 — Range, 10 — Minimum, and 11 — Maximum. These statistics for the grouped data of junior fiction issues (JUFIC) are given in Figure 17.8.

```
MEAN        4.801    MEDIAN        4.337    MODE       3.000
STD DEV     2.103    SKEWNESS      1.005    RANGE      9.000
MINIMUM     2.000    MAXIMUM      11.000

VALID CASES  221     MISSING CASES    13
```

Figure 17.8: Statistics relating to junior fiction issues
(based on grouped data)

Note that the statistics are given in terms of the code numbers for the groups of data and not for the raw data. Figure 17.9 gives the same statistics for the JUFIC data before it was re-coded into groups and, in this case, the statistics relate to the numbers recorded as raw data.

```
JUFIC       NO OF JUNIOR FICTION ISSUES

MEAN      107.688    MEDIAN       93.875    MODE      74.000
STD DEV    51.861    SKEWNESS      1.012    RANGE    233.000
MINIMUM    26.000    MAXIMUM     259.000

VALID CASES  221     MISSING CASES    13
```

Figure 17.9: Statistics relating to junior fiction issues
(based on raw data)

7   One procedure card — and one only — must precede the READ INPUT DATA card. Other procedure cards may follow the READ INPUT DATA card. For example, Figure 17.10 shows lines 33-35 of the program requesting the printout of a SCATTERGRAM of the data on fiction and non-fiction issues and specifying Option 2 (to exclude missing values) and Statistics 1 (Pearson's correlation coefficient), 3 (the significance level of the correlation coefficient) and 4 (the standard error of the estimate).

8   The CROSSTABS procedure, requested in line 36 of the program and shown in Figure 17.11, provides a cross-tabulation between

205

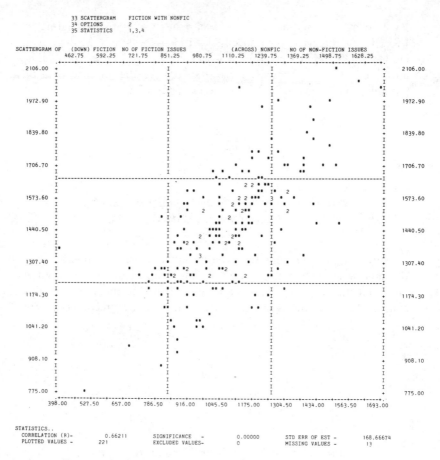

Figure 17:10: Scattergram of fiction with non-fiction issues

two variables — in this case the junior fiction issues and the day of the week. Note that each cell of the table includes figures for:

i the actual number of observations (count) for the day specified at the top of the column and the number of issues specified at the left-hand end of the row;

36 CROSSTABS   TABLES=JUFIC BY DAY

```
* * * * * * * * * * * * * * * * * * *  C R O S S T A B U L A T I O N  O F  * * * * * * * * * * * * *
   JUFIC      GROUPED JUNIOR FICTION ISSUES                        BY  DAY        DAY OF WEEK

                     DAY
             COUNT  I
             ROW PCT IMONDAY   TUESDAY  WEDNESDA THURSDAY FRIDAY   SATURDAY  ROW
             COL PCT I                  Y                                    TOTAL
             TOT PCT I    1.I      2.I      3.I      4.I      5.I      6.I
JUFIC        --------I--------I--------I--------I--------I--------I--------I
             2.  I    4 I     1 I    9 I    1 I    1 I    0 I    16
026-050      I 25.0 I   6.3 I  56.3 I   6.3 I   6.3 I   0.0 I   7.2
             I 11.4 I   2.6 I  23.7 I   2.7 I   2.6 I   0.0 I
             I  1.8 I   0.5 I   4.1 I   0.5 I   0.5 I   0.0 I
             -I--------I--------I--------I--------I--------I--------I
             3.  I    7 I    13 I   13 I    7 I   15 I    1 I    56
051-075      I 12.5 I  23.2 I  23.2 I  12.5 I  26.8 I   1.8 I  25.3
             I 20.0 I  34.2 I  34.2 I  18.9 I  39.5 I   2.9 I
             I  3.2 I   5.9 I   5.9 I   3.2 I   6.8 I   0.5 I
             -I--------I--------I--------I--------I--------I--------I
             4.  I   12 I    10 I    5 I    6 I   11 I    2 I    46
076-100      I 26.1 I  21.7 I  10.9 I  13.0 I  23.9 I   4.3 I  20.8
             I 34.3 I  26.3 I  13.2 I  16.2 I  28.9 I   5.7 I
             I  5.4 I   4.5 I   2.3 I   2.7 I   5.0 I   0.9 I
             -I--------I--------I--------I--------I--------I--------I
             5.  I    8 I     7 I    2 I   12 I    5 I    6 I    40
101-125      I 20.0 I  17.5 I   5.0 I  30.0 I  12.5 I  15.0 I  18.1
             I 22.9 I  18.4 I   5.3 I  32.4 I  13.2 I  17.1 I
             I  3.6 I   3.2 I   0.9 I   5.4 I   2.3 I   2.7 I
             -I--------I--------I--------I--------I--------I--------I
             6.  I    1 I     1 I    2 I    7 I    5 I    7 I    23
126-150      I  4.3 I   4.3 I   8.7 I  30.4 I  21.7 I  30.4 I  10.4
             I  2.9 I   2.6 I   5.3 I  18.9 I  13.2 I  20.0 I
             I  0.5 I   0.5 I   0.9 I   3.2 I   2.3 I   3.2 I
             -I--------I--------I--------I--------I--------I--------I
             7.  I    0 I     2 I    3 I    2 I    1 I    3 I    11
151-175      I  0.0 I  18.2 I  27.3 I  18.2 I   9.1 I  27.3 I   5.0
             I  0.0 I   5.3 I   7.9 I   5.4 I   2.6 I   8.6 I
             I  0.0 I   0.9 I   1.4 I   0.9 I   0.5 I   1.4 I
             -I--------I--------I--------I--------I--------I--------I
             8.  I    2 I     2 I    3 I    1 I    0 I    3 I    11
176-200      I 18.2 I  18.2 I  27.3 I   9.1 I   0.0 I  27.3 I   5.0
             I  5.7 I   5.3 I   7.9 I   2.7 I   0.0 I   8.6 I
             I  0.9 I   0.9 I   1.4 I   0.5 I   0.0 I   1.4 I
             -I--------I--------I--------I--------I--------I--------I
             9.  I    0 I     0 I    1 I    0 I    0 I    8 I    9
201-225      I  0.0 I   0.0 I  11.1 I   0.0 I   0.0 I  88.9 I   4.1
             I  0.0 I   0.0 I   2.6 I   0.0 I   0.0 I  22.9 I
             I  0.0 I   0.0 I   0.5 I   0.0 I   0.0 I   3.6 I
             -I--------I--------I--------I--------I--------I--------I
             10.  I    1 I    2 I    0 I    1 I    0 I    2 I    6
226-250      I 16.7 I  33.3 I   0.0 I  16.7 I   0.0 I  33.3 I   2.7
             I  2.9 I   5.3 I   0.0 I   2.7 I   0.0 I   5.7 I
             I  0.5 I   0.9 I   0.0 I   0.5 I   0.0 I   0.9 I
             -I--------I--------I--------I--------I--------I--------I
             11.  I    0 I    0 I    0 I    0 I    0 I    3 I    3
251-275      I  0.0 I   0.0 I   0.0 I   0.0 I   0.0 I 100.0 I   1.4
             I  0.0 I   0.0 I   0.0 I   0.0 I   0.0 I   8.6 I
             I  0.0 I   0.0 I   0.0 I   0.0 I   0.0 I   1.4 I
             -I--------I--------I--------I--------I--------I--------I
             COLUMN    35      38      38      37      38      35     221
             TOTAL    15.8    17.2    17.2    16.7    17.2    15.8   100.0
NUMBER OF MISSING OBSERVATIONS =    13
```

Figure 17:11: Cross-tabulation of grouped fiction issues by day of week

ii the percentage of the total number of observations of the number of issues specified at the left-hand end of the row;

iii the percentage of the total number of observations for the day specified at the top of the column;

iv the percentage of the grand total of observations.

Actual totals and percentages are given also for each day of the week and each group of numbers of issues.

9   It is possible to select sub-groups of data from the data collected and recorded in the file. The instruction in line 37 (Figure 17.12) requests the computer to include data only if it relates to April or May, ie the variable name (MONTH) is set equal to the value labels 04 or 05 — utilizing appropriate logic to define the interest in either of the two months.

The star preceding the SELECT IF instruction signifies that the selection process applies only to this particular operation and not to any other procedures which may follow. A SELECT IF command that is not preceded by a star would affect all subsequent procedures.

```
37 *SELECT IF       (MONTH EQ 04 OR 05)
```

*Figure 17.12: *SELECT IF command*

10   Having selected data relating only to April and May, a scatter-gram is requested — with certain options and statistics — in lines 38-40 in Figure 17.13.

Note that only 45 records have been plotted as a result of the *SELECT IF command — as compared with the complete set of 221 valid records plotted in Figure 17.10.

Note also that, by specifying Option 4, the plot grid lines have been suppressed.

The request in line 40 of the program for statistics has resulted in the information that the Pearson correlation coefficient is 0.71691 with a very high level of significance (printed as 0.00000) and that the standard error of the estimate is 167.18384.

11   A cross-tabulation of the junior fiction issues by day of the week, again for April and May only, is shown in Figure 17.14, in res-ponse to lines 41-44 of the program.

In this case, the row percentages, column percentages and total percentages have been omitted from the table, having been supressed

```
41 *SELECT IF    (MONTH EQ 04 OR 05)
42 CROSSTABS     TABLES=JUFIC BY DAY
43 OPTIONS       3,4,5
44 STATISTICS    1
```

```
***************** C R O S S T A B U L A T I O N   O F **********
   JUFIC   GROUPED JUNIOR FICTION ISSUES        BY  DAY    DAY OF WEEK

                 DAY
           COUNT I
                 IMONDAY  TUESDAY  WEDNESDA THURSDAY FRIDAY   SATURDAY  ROW
                 I                 Y                                   TOTAL
                 I    1.I      2.I      3.I      4.I     5.I      6.I
 JUFIC    --------I--------I--------I--------I--------I--------I--------I
               2. I    0  I    0  I    1  I    0  I    0  I    0  I       1
          026-050 I       I       I       I       I       I       I     2.2
                 -I--------I--------I--------I--------I--------I--------I
               3. I    1  I    1  I    2  I    1  I    2  I    0  I       7
          051-075 I       I       I       I       I       I       I    15.6
                 -I--------I--------I--------I--------I--------I--------I
               4. I    4  I    2  I    3  I    1  I    3  I    0  I      13
          076-100 I       I       I       I       I       I       I    28.9
                 -I--------I--------I--------I--------I--------I--------I
               5. I    0  I    3  I    1  I    2  I    0  I    0  I       6
          101-125 I       I       I       I       I       I       I    13.3
                 -I--------I--------I--------I--------I--------I--------I
               6. I    0  I    0  I    0  I    3  I    2  I    2  I       7
          126-150 I       I       I       I       I       I       I    15.6
                 -I--------I--------I--------I--------I--------I--------I
               7. I    0  I    1  I    1  I    2  I    0  I    0  I       4
          151-175 I       I       I       I       I       I       I     8.9
                 -I--------I--------I--------I--------I--------I--------I
               8. I    1  I    0  I    0  I    0  I    0  I    2  I       3
          176-200 I       I       I       I       I       I       I     6.7
                 -I--------I--------I--------I--------I--------I--------I
               9. I    0  I    0  I    1  I    0  I    0  I    0  I       1
          201-225 I       I       I       I       I       I       I     2.2
                 -I--------I--------I--------I--------I--------I--------I
              10. I    0  I    2  I    0  I    0  I    0  I    1  I       3
          226-250 I       I       I       I       I       I       I     6.7
                 =I========I========I========I========I========I========I
          COLUMN       6        9        9        9        7        5        45
          TOTAL      13.3     20.0     20.0     20.0     15.6     11.1     100.0

 54 OUT OF     54 (100.0%) OF THE VALID CELLS HAVE EXPECTED CELL FREQUENCY LESS THAN 5.0.
 MINIMUM EXPECTED CELL FREQUENCY =  0.111
 CHI SQUARE =   51.67450 WITH  40 DEGREES OF FREEDOM    SIGNIFICANCE =  0.1022
 NUMBER OF MISSING OBSERVATIONS =      7
```

*Figure 17.14: Cross-tabulation of selected junior fiction issues
by day of week*

by Options 3, 4 and 5 specified in line 43. In line 44, a value of chi-square is requested and the detail below the table shows χ^2 to be 51.67450, which has a significance level of only 0.1. That would suggest that the pattern of junior fiction issues does not depend on the day of the week but it is pointed out that all the cells have an expected frequency of less than 5 (see comment in Chapter 9 on minimum acceptable values in cells).

12   Having completed all the procedures, control is switched back from **SPSS** to the computer monitoring system and the program is ended with the following cards:

210

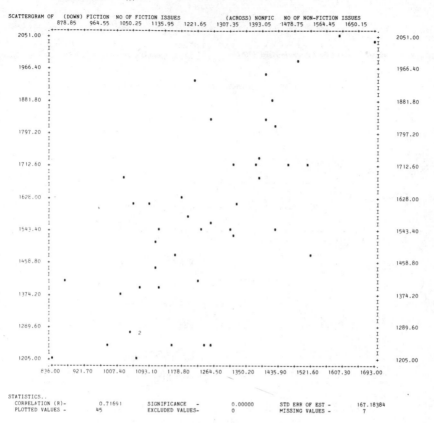

```
            38 SCATTERGRAM   FICTION WITH NONFIC
            39 OPTIONS       2,4
            40 STATISTICS    1,3,4
```

Figure 17.13: Scattergram of selected fiction with non-fiction issues

FINISH
$ENDFILE
$SIG

A complete listing of the program that generated the above examples of the application of SPSS (apart from signing on and off the computer) is shown in Figure 17.15. In a complete study, the data for FICTION, NONFIC, and JUNOFIC would be grouped by recoding in the same way as has been illustrated for the JUFIC data. It is important that the order of the control cards, specified in the rules for the system, is strictly adhered to.

```
$RUN *SPSS 8=LIBISSUES 6=*SINK*@MCC
RUN NAME        LIBRARY ISSUE STATISTICS
PAGESIZE        NOEJECT
DATA LIST       FIXED(1)/1 DAY 1  MONTH 6-7  FICTION 11-14  NONFIC 21-24
                JUFIC 31-33  JUNOFIC 41-43  PERSON 78-80
INPUT MEDIUM    DISK
N OF CASES      234
RECODE          JUFIC (001 THRU 025=01) (026 THRU 050=02) (051 THRU 075=03)
                (076 THRU 100=04) (101 THRU 125=05) (126 THRU 150=06)
                (151 THRU 175=07) (176 THRU 200=08) (201 THRU 225=09)
                (226 THRU 250=10) (251 THRU 275=11) (276 THRU 300=12)
                (999=99)
VAR LABELS      DAY,DAY OF WEEK/
                MONTH,MONTH/
                FICTION,NO OF FICTION ISSUES/
                NONFIC,NO OF NON-FICTION ISSUES/
                JUFIC,GROUPED JUNIOR FICTION ISSUES/
                JUNOFIC,NO OF JUNIOR NON-FICTION ISSUES/
                PERSON,IDENTIFYING RESPONSE NUMBER/
VALUE LABELS    DAY (1) MONDAY  (2) TUESDAY  (3) WEDNESDAY  (4) THURSDAY
                (5) FRIDAY  (6) SATURDAY  (9) NO DATA/
                MONTH (01) JAN  (02) FEB  (03) MAR  (04) APR  (05) MAY  (06) JUN
                (07) JUL  (08) AUG  (09) SEP  (10) OCT  (11) NOV  (12) DEC
                (99) NO DATA/
                FICTION  (9999) NO DATA/
                NONFIC  (9999) NO DATA/
                JUFIC (01) 001-025  (02) 026-050  (03) 051-075  (04) 076-100
                (05) 101-125  (06) 126-150  (07) 151-175  (08) 176-200
                (09) 201-225  (10) 226-250  (11) 251-275  (12) 276-300
                (99) NO DATA/
                JUNOFIC (999) NO DATA/
MISSING VALUES  DAY(9)/MONTH,JUFIC(99)/JUNOFIC(999)/FICTION,NONFIC(9999)
FREQUENCIES     GENERAL=JUFIC
OPTIONS         6
STATISTICS      1,3,4,5,8,9,10,11
READ INPUT DATA
SCATTERGRAM     FICTION WITH NONFIC
OPTIONS         2
STATISTICS      1,3,4
CROSSTABS       TABLES=JUFIC BY DAY
*SELECT IF      (MONTH EQ 04 OR 05)
SCATTERGRAM     FICTION WITH NONFIC
OPTIONS         2,4
STATISTICS      1,3,4
*SELECT IF      (MONTH EQ 04 OR 05)
CROSSTABS       TABLES=JUFIC BY DAY
OPTIONS         3,4,5
STATISTICS      1
FINISH
```

Figure 17.15: Complete listing of SPSS program for the analyses described in this chapter

211

This chapter is only a brief introduction to the use of a computer package for carrying out statistical analyses — as, indeed, is the whole work to the use of statistics. Nevertheless, it is hoped that the reader will have gained sufficient insight into the value and methodology of statistics to be encouraged to explore the subject further and to apply it to everyday problems of managing library and information services and to research in the field of library and information science.

FURTHER READING

1 Busha, C H and Harter, S P *Research methods in librarianship: techniques and interpretation* Academic Press, 1980.

2 Campbell, S K *Flaws and fallacies in statistical thinking* Prentice-Hall, 1974.

3 Carpenter, R L and Vasu, E S *Statistical methods for librarians* American Library Association, 1978.

4 Ehrenberg, A S C *Data reduction: analysing and interpreting statistical data* Wiley, 1975.

5 Federer, W T *Statistics and society: data collection and interpretation* Dekker, 1973.

6 Harper, W M *Statistics* MacDonald & Evans, 4th ed, 1982.

7 Hoel, P G *Elementary statistics* Wiley, 4th ed, 1976.

8 Hull, C H and Nie, N H *SPSS update 7-9: new procedures and facilities for releases 7-9* McGraw-Hill, 1981.

9 Huff, D *How to lie with statistics* Penguin, 1973.

10 Kendall, M G and Buckland, W H *A dictionary of statistical terms* Longman, 3rd ed, 1971.

11 Kimble, G A *How to use (and misuse) statistics* Prentice-Hall, 1978.

12 Lindley, D V and Miller, J C P *Cambridge elementary statistical tables* CUP, 1966.

13 Line, M B *Library surveys: an introduction to the use, planning, procedure and presentation of surveys* Bingley, 2nd ed, 1982.

14 Marchant, M P et al *SPSS as a library research tool* School of Library and Information Sciences, Occasional Research Paper No 1, Brigham Young University, 1977.

15 Nie, N H et al *SPSS: statistical package for the social sciences* McGraw-Hill, 2nd ed, 1975.

16 Pearson, E S and Hartley, H O *Biometrika tables for statisticians* Volume I, Griffin, 3rd ed, 1976.

17 Simpson, I S *Basic statistics for librarians* Bingley, 1st ed, 1975.

18 Wallis, W A and Roberts, H V *Statistics: a new approach* Methuen, 1957.

19 Yeomans, K A *Statistics for the social scientist: 1 Introducing statistics* Penguin, 1968.

20 Yeomans, K A *Statistics for the social sciences: 2 Applied statistics* Penguin, 1968.

ANSWERS TO EXAMPLES

Note that precise answers will be affected by the extent to which numbers have been rounded and therefore small discrepancies should be ignored.

2.1	(a) 20	(b) 20	(c) 19.53
2.2	(a) 3	(b) 4	(c) 4.83
2.3	(a) 2	(b) 3	(c) 2.91
2.4	(a) 65	(b) 65	(c) 62.4
2.5	(a) 111-120	(b) 121.7	(c) 127.59
2.6	(1.5) (a) 36-40	(b) 38.28	(c) 37.87
	(1.6) (a) 16-20.99	(b) 22.17	(c) 22.94

3.1	(a) 1.96	(b) 1.5	(c) −0.24
3.2	(a) 2.70	(b) 1.75	(c) +0.68
3.3	(a) 1.73	(b) 1.0	(c) +0.53
3.4	(a) 9.50	(b) 5.0	(c) −0.27
3.5	(a) 33.78	(b) 20.0	(c) +0.36

4.1	14.66; 4.42	
4.2	(1) 28.6	(2) 3.57: 1.60

5.1 $26.82 < \mu < 30.38$; between 11533 and 13063 quotations
5.2 $30.73 < \mu < 49.27$; £271; $n = 35$
5.3 $28.95 < \mu < 40.94$; 41.28
5.4 $2.62 < \mu < 5.38$; 2.49
5.5 11.07 inches

6.1 373
6.2 1947; 4719
6.5 1150

6.6 (a) 3275 (b) 15875
6.7 1812; 2207
6.8 3310; 1759
6.9 (a) 20 (b) 126
6.10 (a) 0.3 (b) 0.26
6.11 0.186
6.12 0.09
6.13 44
6.14 3.1; 163
6.15 2; 0.271
6.16 £84; 23 weeks in the year
6.17 0.0176

7.1 $Z = 3.0$ Significant difference between sample and population at 0.01 level
7.2 $t = 1.686$ No significant difference
7.3 $t = 11.09$ Demand is significantly different in the winter (at 0.01 level)
7.4 $t = 2.754$ Illustrated paperbacks were significantly dearer (at 0.05 level)
7.5 $t = 2.80$ Demand is significantly greater in August (at 0.05 level)
7.6 $\bar{X} = 15.667$ $t = 0.607$ No significant difference
7.7 $t = 2.539$ User's longer time is significant at 0.05 level
7.8 $t = 0.259$ No significant difference
7.9 $t = -2.18$ Number of books per shelf is significantly different at 0.05 level
7.10 $t = 0.573$ No significant difference
7.11 $F = 1.747$ No significant difference
7.12 $F = 3.653$ Dispersions are significantly different at 0.05 level

9.1 $\chi^2 = 9.39$ Increase is significant at 0.01 level
9.2 $\chi^2 = 0.917$ No significant difference
9.3 $\chi^2 = 1.599$ No significant difference
9.4 $\chi^2 = 47.33$ Sex of authors is significantly different at 0.01 level
9.5 $\chi^2 = 0.191$ No significant difference
9.6 $\chi^2 = 3.223$ No significant difference
9.7 $\chi^2 = 0.136$ No significant difference
9.8 $\chi^2 = 52.77$ Work groups are significantly different at 0.01 level
9.9 $\chi^2 = 0.00016$ No significant difference

11.1 (a) (i) 209.5   (ii) 185.4
     (b) 187.7
11.2 144.5; No (I = 143.6); 7p
11.3 (a) (i) 113.1   (ii) 127.1   (iii) 111.3
     (b) Books 43.48; Total 46.7
11.5 (a) 124.2
     (b) 119.4
11.6 (a) Staff: 129.1; 111.3; 102.5
     (b) Books: 113.0; 115.4; 110.0

12.1 3.825 3.945 3.9625 4.015 4.0375 4.045 4.09
     6.93%; 1.16%
12.2 42.17 40.67 43.83 43.33 40.33 40.5 38.17 36.0 35.67 36.0
     35.67 35.17 31.67
      5.58 −6.25 52.42 −11.83 −7.415 −21.335 −8.085 1.165
     46.165 −18.835 −4.42 −13.42
12.3 26 29 33 40 47 56 65
     3.5; 9.0; 6.5
12.4 28328 29249 29475 30970 32498 34356 36269 38523
     39183
     38.32%
12.5 7.4   8.8   10.4   14.8   19.0   25.2   31.2   40.4   45.2

13.1 F = 2.23 Not significant
13.2 F = 1.46 Not significant
13.3 F = 7.24 Dispersions are significantly different at 0.05 level

15.1 r = 0.885 t = 6.58   Significant at 0.01 level
     ρ = 0.892 t = 6.84   Significant at 0.01 level
15.2 r = 0.385 t = 1.25   Not significant
     ρ = 0.046 t = 0.14   Not significant
15.3 r = −0.871 t = −4.34   Significant at 0.01 level
     ρ = −0.804 t = −3.31   Significant at 0.05 level
15.4 r = 0.861 t = 5.35   Significant at 0.01 level
     ρ = 0.769 t = 3.8   Significant at 0.01 level
15.5 r = 0.938 t = 7.16   Significant at 0.01 level
     ρ = 0.933 t = 6.86   Significant at 0.01 level
15.6 r = −0.578 t = −1.735   Not significant
     ρ = −0.69 t = −2.33   Not significant
15.7 r = 0.719 t = 10.08   Significant at 0.01 level

16.1 939   Standard error 228
16.2 49   Standard error 26
16.3 5.61   Standard error 1.64
16.4 97   Standard error 37
16.5 (a) 8950   Standard error 4027
     (b) £43.41 Standard error £12.01
16.6 (a) 805   Standard error 381
     (b) 737   Standard error 481

Appendix 1

MATHEMATICAL METHODS

Experience has shown that readers are not always familiar with mathematical symbols and conventions, Greek letters, and basic arithmetic operations. It is hoped that the following notes will provide the necessary revision and/or clarification.

Symbols: Arithmetic

$=$ means 'is equal to' (eg $2 + 3 = 5$)

$>$ means 'is greater than' (eg $6 > 2$)

$\geqslant$ means 'is greater than or equal to' (eg $x \geqslant 2$ means that x has a value of 2 or more)

$<$ means 'is less than' (eg $6 < 10$)

$\leqslant$ means 'is less than or equal to' (eg $x \leqslant 2$ means that x has a value of 2 or less)

$\div$ means 'divided by' (eg $12 \div 3 = 4$)

$-$ means 'divided by' if used thus: $\dfrac{12}{3} = 4$

$-$ otherwise means 'subtract' (eg $12 - 3 = 9$)

. is a decimal point (eg 2.5 means two point five or two and a half)

. may also mean 'multiplied by' (eg $n \cdot x$ means n multiplied by x) (The product of two numbers may also be represented simply by nx without the intervening point)

$\%$ means 'per hundred' (eg 95% is 95 out of 100)

x^2 means 'multiply x by itself' (eg $3^2 = 3 \times 3 = 9$)

x^3 means 'multiply x by itself and multiply the answer by x (eg $2^3 = 2 \times 2 \times 2 = 4 \times 2 = 8$)

$\sqrt{x}$ means 'that value which, when squared, is equal to x' (eg $\sqrt{9} = 3$)

Symbols: Greek
The following are letters of the Greek alphabet together with phonetic pronunciations:

μ mu

χ khi

ρ rho

σ sigma (lower case)

Σ sigma (upper case). Σ is used in statistics to mean 'add together'. Thus:

ΣX means 'add together the various values of X'. So, if 2, 3 and 5 are three values of X:

$$\Sigma X = 2 + 3 + 5 = 10$$

ΣX^2 means 'square each value of X and then add together the various squared values of X'. So, if 2, 3 and 5 are three values of X:

$$\Sigma X^2 = 2^2 + 3^2 + 5^2$$
$$= 4 + 9 + 25$$
$$= 38$$

$(\Sigma X)^2$ means 'add together the various values of X and then square the result'. So, if 2, 3 and 5 are three values of X:

$$(\Sigma X)^2 = (2 + 3 + 5)^2$$
$$= 10^2$$
$$= 100$$

ΣXY means 'multiply each value of X by the corresponding value of Y and add together the various products'. So, if 2, 3 and 5 are three values of X and 6, 7 and 4 are three corresponding values of Y:

$$\Sigma XY = (2 \times 6) + (3 \times 7) + (5 \times 4)$$
$$= 12 + 21 + 20$$
$$= 53$$

$\sum_{0}^{3} P(x)$ means 'add together all the various values of $P(x)$ from $x = 0$ to $x = 3$ inclusive, ie $P(0) + P(1) + P(2) + P(3)$.

Symbols: other

e is a fixed number known as the 'exponential constant' and is equal to 2.718.

f is used to represent 'frequency'. A subscript indicates whether the frequency was 'observed' (f_o) or 'expected' (f_e).

$n!$ is 'factorial n' and means: $n \times (n - 1) \times (n - 2) \ldots \times 1$. So, if $n = 3, n! = 3 \times 2 \times 1 = 6$.

$(n - r)!$ is 'factorial n minus r' and means: $(n - r) \times (n - r - 1) \times (n - r - 2) \ldots \times 1$. So, if $n = 6$ and $r = 2$, $(n - r)! = 4 \times 3 \times 2 \times 1 = 24$.

$\overline{X}$ is referred to as 'X bar'.

Operations

BOMDAS Remember the mnemonic, giving the order in which arithmetic operations must be performed.

First, work out whatever is contained in **B**rackets:

$$(9 + 6) - 2 \times 3 = 15 - 2 \times 3$$

Then, **M**ultiply or **D**ivide:

$$15 - 2 \times 3 = 15 - 6$$

Finally, **A**dd or **S**ubtract:

$$15 - 6 = 9$$

By following these basic rules, an all-too-common error will be avoided. To say that $15 - 2 \times 3 = 13 \times 3 = 39$ *is wrong!*

Multiplication

$n\overline{X}; pq;$
$(n - 1)(n - 2)$ all mean that the two factors are multiplied together. Thus:

$$\text{if } n = 20 \text{ and } \overline{X} = 4.5, n\overline{X} = 20 \times 4.5 = 90$$
$$\text{if } p = \tfrac{3}{4} \text{ and } q = \tfrac{1}{4}, pq = \tfrac{3}{4} \times \tfrac{1}{4} = \tfrac{3}{16}$$
$$\text{if } n = 5, (n - 1)(n - 2) = 4 \times 3 = 12$$

$n\overline{X}^2$ means 'square the value of $\overline{X}$ and then multiply by the value of n'. Thus:

$$\text{if } n = 10 \text{ and } \overline{X} = 4, n\overline{X}^2 = 10 \times 4^2 = 10 \times 16 = 160$$

Exponential

e^x means 'multiply e together x times'. Thus:

$$\text{if } x = 2, e^x = e^2 = 2.718^2 = 2.718 \times 2.718 = 7.388$$

e^{-x} is the same as $\dfrac{1}{e^x}$. Thus:

$$\text{if } x = 2, e^{-x} = \frac{1}{e^2} = \frac{1}{2.718^2} = \frac{1}{7.388} = 0.135$$

Accuracy

If calculators are used for performing calculations, they will often give more figures in the answer than is justifiable. To give an answer as 24.4652 implies an accuracy to 6 significant figures. The number of decimal places is not important − 2446.52 also implies an accuracy to 6 significant figures.

If such high accuracy is not justified, the figures can be rounded. If the final digit is 6 or more, the number is rounded up:

eg 24.46 becomes 24.5

If the final digit is 4 or less, the number is rounded down:

eg 24.4652 becomes 24.465

If the final digit is a 5, it is customary to round to an even number:

eg 24.465 is rounded to 24.46
    24.475 is rounded to 24.48

If 24.4652 is rounded, it becomes:

24.465 to 5 significant figures
24.46 to 4 significant figures
24.5   to 3 significant figures
24   to 2 significant figures

To give an answer as 24.5 implies that the true answer lies between 24.45 and 24.55. The absolute error is therefore 0.05. From this, the relative error is determined from the expression:

$$\text{Relative error} = \frac{\text{Absolute error}}{\text{Approximate value}} \times 100\%$$

$$= \frac{0.05}{24.5} \times 100\%$$

$$= 0.2\%$$

To give an answer as 24500 gives the same relative error since the absolute error is 50 (the true answer being between 24450 and 24550). Therefore:

$$\text{Relative error} = \frac{50}{24500} \times 100\%$$

$$= 0.2\%$$

So, the relative error is not a question of the number of decimal places in an answer but the number of significant figures. If, for example, an answer of 24.5 is rounded to 24, there are now only two

222

significant figures instead of 3 and the answer implies that the true answer lies between 23.5 and 24.5. The relative error in this case is:

$$\frac{0.5}{24} \times 100\%$$

$$= 2.08\%$$

It is not advisable to round figures too much at intermediate stages of a calculation since the errors caused by so doing will be additive. Consequently, the final answer is not going to be as accurate as it would be if rounding to a justifiable degree of accuracy is left to the last stage of the calculation. On the other hand, there is no point in retaining an unnecessary number of significant figures throughout a calculation.

Appendix 2

SYMBOLS USED
(See also Appendix 1)

a = intercept of line of regression of y on x
a^* = intercept of line of regression of x on y
b = gradient of line of regression of y on x
b^* = gradient of line of regression of x on y
χ^2 = distribution used in statistical tests involving qualitative data
D = difference between rankings of two variables
f_e = expected frequency
f_o = observed frequency
F = ratio of variances of two samples
I = index number
μ = population mean
n = number of observations in a sample
N = number of observations in a population
p = probability of success
p_o = price in base year
p_n = price in given year
$P(x)$ = probability of x being observed
q = probability of failure
q_o = quantity in base year
q_n = quantity in given year
r = Pearson correlation coefficient
ρ = Spearman correlation coefficient
s = standard deviation in a sample
s_D = standard error of difference between sample means when only sample standard deviations are known
$s_{\bar{X}}$ = standard error of the mean (when σ is not known)
s^2 = variance in a sample
σ = standard deviation in a population
σ_D = standard error of difference between sample means when population standard deviations are known

224

$\sigma_{\overline{X}}$ = standard error of the mean (when σ is known)

σ^2 = variance in a population

Σ = sign of addition

t = distribution used in statistical tests involving small samples of quantitative data

x = value of a variable with respect to the X axis for an observation in a population

X = value of a variable with respect to the X axis for an observation in a sample

$\overline{X}$ = mean value of X in a sample

$\overline{\overline{X}}$ = mean value of the means – or 'grand mean'

y = value of a variable with respect to the Y axis for an observation in a population

Y = value of a variable with respect to the Y axis for an observation in a sample

$\overline{Y}$ = mean value of Y in a sample

Z = distribution used in statistical tests involving large samples of quantitative data

Appendix 3

FORMULAE USED

These formulae are presented in the order in which they occur in the text.

1 Population mean $= \mu = \dfrac{\Sigma x}{N}$

2 Population standard deviation $= \sigma = \sqrt{\dfrac{\Sigma(x - \mu^2)}{N}}$ or $\sqrt{\dfrac{\Sigma x^2}{N} - \mu^2}$

3 Sample mean $= \bar{X} = \dfrac{\Sigma X}{n}$

4 Skewness $= \dfrac{\text{Mean} - \text{Mode}}{\text{Standard deviation}}$

5 Skewness $= \dfrac{3 \times (\text{Mean} - \text{Median})}{\text{Standard deviation}}$

6 Sample standard deviation $= s = \sqrt{\dfrac{\Sigma(X - \bar{X})^2}{n - 1}}$ or $\sqrt{\dfrac{\Sigma X^2 - n\bar{X}^2}{n - 1}}$

7 Standard error of the mean (if σ is known) $= \sigma_{\bar{X}} = \dfrac{\sigma}{\sqrt{n}}$

8 Standard error of the mean (if σ is not known) $= s_{\bar{X}} = \dfrac{s}{\sqrt{n}}$

9 Relationship between σ and s: $\sigma = \sqrt{\dfrac{n}{n - 1}} \times s$

10 Precision of sample $= \dfrac{\sqrt{n}}{\sigma}$ or $\dfrac{\sqrt{n}}{s}$

11 Standard error of probability of success $= \sqrt{\dfrac{pq}{n}}$

12 Probability of observing a variable x in Binomial distribution:

$$P(x) = \frac{n!}{x!(n-x)!} p^x q^{n-x}$$

13 Mean of Binomial distribution $= \mu = np$

14 Standard deviation of Binomial distribution $= \sigma = \sqrt{npq}$

15 Probability of observing a variable x in a Poisson distribution:

$$P(x) = e^{-\mu} \cdot \frac{\mu^x}{x!}$$

16 Mean of Poisson distribution $= \mu = np$

17 Standard deviation of Poisson distribution $= \sigma = \sqrt{np} = \sqrt{\mu}$

18 Standard normal distribution:

$$Z = \frac{x - \mu}{\sigma} \quad \text{for a population}$$

$$= \frac{X - \bar{X}}{s} \quad \text{for a sample}$$

$$= \frac{\bar{X} - \mu}{\sigma_{\bar{X}}} \text{ or } \frac{\bar{X} - \mu}{s_{\bar{X}}} \quad \text{for distribution of sample means}$$

$$= \frac{\bar{X}_1 - \bar{X}_2}{\sigma_D} \quad \text{for two samples}$$

19 Standard error of sampling distribution of differences between two means is given by:

$$\sigma_D{}^2 = \sigma_{\bar{X}_1}{}^2 + \sigma_{\bar{X}_2}{}^2 = \frac{\sigma_1{}^2}{n_1} + \frac{\sigma_2{}^2}{n_2}$$

$$\text{or} \quad s_D{}^2 = s_{\bar{X}_1}{}^2 + s_{\bar{X}_2}{}^2 = \frac{s_1{}^2}{n_1} + \frac{s_2{}^2}{n_2}$$

20 Student's distribution: $t = \dfrac{\bar{X} - \mu}{s_{\bar{X}}}$

21 F distribution: $F = \dfrac{s_1{}^2}{s_2{}^2}$ where $s_1 > s_2$

22 Chi-square distribution $\chi^2 = \sum \dfrac{(f_o - f_e)^2}{f_e}$

23 Simple aggregative index: $I = \dfrac{\Sigma p_n}{\Sigma p_o} \times 100$

24 Weighted aggregative index:

$$\text{Base year weighting } I = \frac{\Sigma p_n q_o}{\Sigma p_o q_o} \times 100$$

$$\text{Given year weighting } I = \frac{\Sigma p_n q_n}{\Sigma p_o q_n} \times 100$$

25 Pearson correlation coefficient $= r = \dfrac{\Sigma XY - n\overline{X}\,\overline{Y}}{\sqrt{(\Sigma X^2 - n\overline{X}^2)(\Sigma Y^2 - n\overline{Y}^2)}}$

26 Spearman correlation coefficient $= \rho = 1 - \dfrac{6\Sigma D^2}{n(n^2 - 1)}$

27 Regression line of y on x: $y = a + bx$

28 Regression coefficient of y on $x = b = \dfrac{\Sigma XY - n\overline{X}\,\overline{Y}}{\Sigma X^2 - n\overline{X}^2}$

29 Regression line of x on y: $x = a^* + b^*y$

30 Regression coefficient of x on $y = b^* = \dfrac{\Sigma XY - n\overline{X}\,\overline{Y}}{\Sigma Y^2 - n\overline{Y}^2}$

31 Standard error about the regression line of y on x =

$$\sqrt{\frac{\Sigma Y^2 - n\overline{Y}^2}{n - 1}} \times \sqrt{1 - r^2}$$

32 Standard error about the regression line of x on y =

$$\sqrt{\frac{\Sigma X^2 - n\overline{X}^2}{n - 1}} \times \sqrt{1 - r^2}$$

Appendix 4

RANDOM NUMBERS

96 35	02 91	66 38	70 86	86 28	20 25	17 09	32 87	77 44	51 87
86 15	83 61	91 90	08 06	57 56	78 05	37 31	34 22	54 20	81 09
51 05	74 64	30 16	16 41	37 19	39 67	26 02	91 53	37 19	24 36
19 37	77 47	25 09	95 35	14 08	79 25	96 92	96 67	61 47	22 41
86 15	93 12	38 72	09 28	16 72	51 16	86 00	50 29	98 91	67 53
21 48	84 79	03 61	25 49	23 46	00 02	18 26	87 34	58 03	66 75
32 02	95 72	53 47	27 80	41 02	51 33	72 62	35 49	35 00	69 44
26 31	71 43	78 13	78 68	27 36	73 54	62 85	29 84	76 26	58 80
81 68	15 26	08 48	55 06	66 75	59 38	55 30	36 23	84 56	94 54
77 81	88 70	99 76	76 23	90 35	68 36	80 24	05 06	13 55	27 68
00 98	35 60	07 80	00 78	09 58	50 40	25 60	00 42	05 22	84 52
14 54	51 59	61 03	17 52	70 18	42 71	90 24	39 92	76 23	00 61
84 35	46 67	32 41	47 84	97 98	17 34	57 17	43 96	79 99	94 82
64 23	84 66	64 68	06 06	03 39	81 00	49 27	83 68	37 90	70 72
52 32	67 59	89 96	89 32	94 88	36 01	89 27	82 59	23 24	68 70
77 74	85 81	62 59	61 78	55 79	74 81	30 90	73 37	89 00	62 34
52 87	20 12	97 06	75 23	92 24	95 62	13 69	20 54	91 35	48 11
39 87	70 70	91 20	90 60	84 36	31 98	61 09	92 70	17 00	81 81
65 22	92 19	20 21	63 52	12 93	94 21	36 00	09 35	17 30	66 99
64 22	18 05	10 47	99 32	16 57	42 78	80 61	17 92	02 38	96 87
38 49	23 61	60 54	69 93	50 54	92 91	66 01	50 42	17 70	44 29
41 49	13 86	04 31	90 31	70 59	73 35	16 35	84 15	88 26	38 63
85 36	10 75	31 10	27 36	54 06	00 59	60 44	23 55	69 94	43 37
70 72	88 69	62 66	96 93	89 46	69 54	91 15	33 92	49 55	26 42
20 23	89 70	55 03	93 50	62 50	91 58	36 61	07 20	12 37	13 25

Appendix 5

t-DISTRIBUTION

Degrees of Freedom	SIGNIFICANCE LEVELS			
	10 (.05,1 tail)	.05 (2 tails)	.02 (.01,1 tail)	.01 (2 tails)
1	6.314	12.706	31.821	63.657
2	2.920	4.303	6.965	9.925
3	2.353	3.182	4.541	5.841
4	2.132	2.776	3.747	4.604
5	2.015	2.571	3.365	4.032
6	1.943	2.447	3.143	3.707
7	1.895	2.365	2.998	3.499
8	1.860	2.306	2.896	3.355
9	1.833	2.262	2.821	3.250
10	1.812	2.228	2.764	3.169
11	1.796	2.201	2.718	3.106
12	1.782	2.179	2.681	3.055
13	1.771	2.160	2.650	3.012
14	1.761	2.145	2.624	2.977
15	1.753	2.131	2.602	2.947
16	1.746	2.120	2.583	2.921
17	1.740	2.110	2.567	2.898
18	1.734	2.101	2.552	2.878
19	1.729	2.093	2.539	2.861
20	1.725	2.086	2.528	2.845
21	1.721	2.080	2.518	2.831
22	1.717	2.074	2.508	1.819
23	1.714	2.069	2.500	2.807
24	1.711	2.064	2.492	2.797
25	1.708	2.060	2.485	2.787
26	1.706	2.056	2.479	2.779
27	1.703	2.052	2.473	2.771
28	1.701	2.048	2.467	2.763
29 or more (equivalent to z)	1.600	2.000	2.300	2.600

Appendix 6

F DISTRIBUTION

0.01 Significance level

ν_N / ν_D	3	4	5	6	7	8	9	10	12	15	20	24	30	40
3	29·46	28·71	28·24	27·91	27·67	27·49	27·35	27·23	27·05	26·87	26·69	26·60	26·51	26·41
4	16·69	15·98	15·52	15·21	14·98	14·80	14·66	14·55	14·37	14·20	14·02	13·93	13·84	13·75
5	12·06	11·39	10·97	10·67	10·46	10·29	10·16	10·05	9·89	9·72	9·55	9·47	9·38	9·29
6	9·78	9·15	8·75	8·47	8·26	8·10	7·98	7·87	7·72	7·56	7·40	7·31	7·23	7·14
7	8·45	7·85	7·46	7·19	6·99	6·84	6·72	6·62	6·47	6·31	6·16	6·07	5·99	5·91
8	7·59	7·01	6·63	6·37	6·18	6·03	5·91	5·81	5·67	5·52	5·36	5·28	5·20	5·12
9	6·99	6·42	6·06	5·80	5·61	5·47	5·35	5·26	5·11	4·96	4·81	4·73	4·65	4·57
10	6·55	5·99	5·64	5·39	5·20	5·06	4·94	4·85	4·71	4·56	4·41	4·33	4·25	4·17
12	5·95	5·41	5·06	4·82	4·64	4·50	4·39	4·30	4·16	4·01	3·86	3·78	3·70	3·62
15	5·42	4·89	4·56	4·32	4·14	4·00	3·89	3·80	3·67	3·52	3·37	3·29	3·21	3·13
20	4·94	4·43	4·10	3·87	3·70	3·56	3·46	3·37	3·23	3·09	2·94	2·86	2·78	2·69
24	4·72	4·22	3·90	3·67	3·50	3·36	3·26	3·17	3·03	2·89	2·74	2·66	2·58	2·49
30	4·51	4·02	3·70	3·47	3·30	3·17	3·07	2·98	2·84	2·70	2·55	2·47	2·39	2·30
40	4·31	3·83	3·51	3·29	3·12	2·99	2·89	2·80	2·66	2·52	2·37	2·29	2·20	2·11

0.05 Significance level

ν_D \ ν_N	3	4	5	6	7	8	9	10	12	15	20	24	30	40
3	9·28	9·12	9·01	8·94	8·89	8·85	8·81	8·79	8·74	8·70	8·66	8·64	8·62	8·59
4	6·59	6·39	6·26	6·16	6·09	6·04	6·00	5·96	5·91	5·86	5·80	5·77	5·75	5·72
5	5·41	5·19	5·05	4·95	4·88	4·82	4·77	4·74	4·68	4·62	4·56	4·53	4·50	4·46
6	4·76	4·53	4·39	4·28	4·21	4·15	4·10	4·06	4·00	3·94	3·87	3·84	3·81	3·77
7	4·35	4·12	3·97	3·87	3·79	3·73	3·68	3·64	3·57	3·51	3·44	3·41	3·38	3·34
8	4·07	3·84	3·69	3·58	3·50	3·44	3·39	3·35	3·28	3·22	3·15	3·12	3·08	3·04
9	3·86	3·63	3·48	3·37	3·29	3·23	3·18	3·14	3·07	3·01	2·94	2·90	2·86	2·83
10	3·71	3·48	3·33	3·22	3·14	3·07	3·02	2·98	2·91	2·85	2·77	2·74	2·70	2·66
12	3·49	3·26	3·11	3·00	2·91	2·85	2·80	2·75	2·69	2·62	2·54	2·51	2·47	2·43
15	3·29	3·06	2·90	2·79	2·71	2·64	2·59	2·54	2·48	2·40	2·33	2·29	2·25	2·20
20	3·10	2·87	2·71	2·60	2·51	2·45	2·39	2·35	2·28	2·20	2·12	2·08	2·04	1·99
24	3·01	2·78	2·62	2·51	2·42	2·36	2·30	2·25	2·18	2·11	2·03	1·98	1·94	1·89
30	2·92	2·69	2·53	2·42	2·33	2·27	2·21	2·16	2·09	2·01	1·93	1·89	1·84	1·79
40	2·84	2·61	2·45	2·34	2·25	2·18	2·12	2·08	2·00	1·92	1·84	1·79	1·74	1·69

Appendix 7

χ^2 DISTRIBUTION

Degrees of Freedom	SIGNIFICANCE LEVELS					
	0.99	0.95	0.10 (.05 in 1 tail)	0.05 (in 2 tails)	0.02 (.01 in 1 tail)	0.01 (in 2 tails)
1	.00157	.00393	2.706	3.841	5.412	6.635
2	.0201	.103	4.605	5.991	7.824	9.210
3	.115	.352	6.251	7.815	9.837	11.340
4	.297	.711	7.779	9.488	11.668	13.277
5	.554	1.145	9.236	11.070	13.388	15.086
6	.872	1.635	10.645	12.592	15.033	16.812
7	1.239	2.167	12.017	14.067	16.622	18.475
8	1.646	2.733	13.362	15.507	18.168	20.090
9	2.088	3.325	14.684	16.919	19.679	21.666
10	2.558	3.940	15.987	18.307	21.161	23.209
11	3.053	4.575	17.275	19.675	22.618	24.725
12	3.571	5.226	18.549	21.026	24.054	26.217
13	4.107	5.892	19.812	22.362	25.472	27.688
14	4.660	6.571	21.064	23.685	26.873	29.141
15	5.229	7.261	22.307	24.996	28.259	30.578
16	5.812	7.962	23.542	26.296	29.633	32.000
17	6.408	8.672	24.769	27.587	30.995	33.409
18	7.015	9.390	25.989	28.869	32.346	34.805
19	7.633	10.117	27.204	30.144	33.687	36.191
20	8.260	10.851	28.412	31.410	35.020	37.566

Appendix 8

$$e^{-x}$$

x	e^{-x}	x	e^{-x}	x	e^{-x}
0	1.0000	1.0	0.3679	2.0	0.1353
0.1	0.9048	1.1	0.3329	2.1	0.1225
0.2	0.8187	1.2	0.3012	2.2	0.1108
0.3	0.7408	1.3	0.2725	2.3	0.1003
0.4	0.6703	1.4	0.2466	2.4	0.0907
0.5	0.6065	1.5	0.2231	2.5	0.0821
0.6	0.5488	1.6	0.2019	2.6	0.0743
0.7	0.4966	1.7	0.1827	2.7	0.0672
0.8	0.4493	1.8	0.1653	2.8	0.0608
0.9	0.4066	1.9	0.1496	2.9	0.0550
3.0	0.0498	4.0	0.0183	5.0	0.0067
3.1	0.0450	4.1	0.0166	5.1	0.0061
3.2	0.0408	4.2	0.0150	5.2	0.0055
3.3	0.0369	4.3	0.0136	5.3	0.0050
3.4	0.0334	4.4	0.0123	5.4	0.0045
3.5	0.0302	4.5	0.0111	5.5	0.0041
3.6	0.0273	4.6	0.0100	5.6	0.0037
3.7	0.0247	4.7	0.0091	5.7	0.0033
3.8	0.0224	4.8	0.0082	5.8	0.0030
3.9	0.0202	4.9	0.0074	5.9	0.0027
6.0	0.0025	7.0	0.0009	8.0	0.0003
6.1	0.0022	7.1	0.0008	8.1	0.0003
6.2	0.0020	7.2	0.0007	8.2	0.0003
6.3	0.0018	7.3	0.0007	8.3	0.0002
6.4	0.0017	7.4	0.0006	8.4	0.0002
6.5	0.0015	7.5	0.0006	8.5	0.0002
6.6	0.0014	7.6	0.0005	8.6	0.0002
6.7	0.0012	7.7	0.0005	8.7	0.0002
6.8	0.0011	7.8	0.0004	8.8	0.0002
6.9	0.0010	7.9	0.0004	8.9	0.0001
9.0	0.0001				
9.1	0.0001				
9.2	0.0001				
9.3	0.0001				
9.4	0.0001				
9.5	0.0001				
9.6	0.0001				
9.7	0.0001				
9.8	0.0001				
9.9	0.0001				

INDEX

Absolute frequency 202
Accuracy 63, 66, 68, 222-223
Addition law of probability 69, 75, 76
Adjusted frequency 203
Analysis of variance 159-163
Area under curve 41-42
Array 17, 34, 36-37
    (see also Linear array)
Averages 30-39, 152-156

Bar charts 113-114
Base year weighting 144
Bias 52, 60, 64
Biased estimates 59
Binomial distribution 74-80

Chain base index 145-146
Charts
    (see Bar charts; Column
    charts; Grouped column
    charts; Pie charts)
Chi-squared test 119-127
Cluster sampling 55
Column charts 110-113
Computer packages 197-212
Confidence limits 63-65, 70-73
Contingency tables 122-125
Correlation 174-186
Correlation coefficients 175
    (see also Pearson; Spearman)

Correlation tables 169-170, 184-186, 205, 207, 210
Cumulative frequency 22-25, 203
Cumulative frequency graphs 23-25, 47
Current year weighting 144
Cyclical variation 153-156

Data 11
    (see also Grouped data;
    Qualitative data; Quanti-
    tative data)
Data lists 198-199
Decile range 48
Definitions 11
Degrees of freedom 97, 120, 123, 161
Deviation
    (see Standard deviation)
Discrepancies 120, 123
Dispersion 40-51, 60, 100
Distribution
    (see Binomial distribution;
    Frequency distribution;
    Normal distribution;
    Poisson distribution;
    Probability distribution;
    Skew distribution; Standard
    normal distribution;

235

Distribution (cont'd)
  Student's distribution;
  Uniform distribution)

Errors 222-223
Expected frequencies 120, 122,
  220
Exponential 81, 220, 221, 234

F-Tests 100-101, 161
Finite population 56
Freedom, degrees of
  (see Degrees of freedom)
Frequency 19, 40, 202-205,
  220
  (see also Cumulative
  frequency; Expected
  frequencies; Observed
  frequencies; Relative
  frequency)
Frequency distributions 40, 57,
  59-60, 86-92
  (see also headings under
  Distribution)
Frequency polygons 22, 27, 34
Frequency tables 18-19, 35, 45

Grand mean 56, 62
Graphs
  (see Cumulative frequency
  graphs; Line graphs; Semi-
  logarithmic graphs; Surface
  graphs)
Greek letters 219-220
Grouped column charts 111-
  113
Grouped data 26, 45
Grouped frequency 26-28
Grouped frequency tables
  26-27, 204

Histograms 20-21, 27, 34, 70,
  204
Historigrams 149-151
Hypothesis, null
  (see Null hypothesis)

Indexes 140-148
Infinite population 56, 62
Interquartile range 46

Line
  (see Regression line; Standard
  error about line)
Line graphs 131-136
Linear array 17-18
Lower quartile 46-47

Mathematical methods 219-
  223
Mean 30, 32-33, 35-37, 40, 56,
  62, 79, 81, 90, 92, 205
Mean value of the means 56-57,
  59-60, 62
Median 30-32, 34, 36-37, 46-47,
  151, 205
Mode 30-31, 34, 49-50, 205
Moving averages 152-156
Multiplication law of probability
  69

Normal distribution 40-42, 50,
  63, 70, 73, 90
  (see also Standard normal
  distribution)
Null hypothesis 85, 87-88, 119

Observed frequencies 119, 220
One-tailed tests 88-90

Parameters 52, 54, 62-66

236

Pearson correlation coefficient 175-178, 180-182
Percentages 109, 141, 208
Pie charts 114-116
Point estimates 62
Poisson distribution 81-82
Population 52, 54, 56, 58-60, 62, 68, 100
Population mean 54, 60, 62, 64, 92
Precision 60
Probability 68-82
Probability distribution 74
Probability of failure 71, 78
Probability of success 71, 78, 81

Qualitative data 13, 105-163
Quantitative data 13, 17-103, 129-193
Quartiles 46-47

Random sampling 53, 59
Range 18, 41, 205
    (see also Decile range;
    Interquartile range;
    Semi-interquartile range)
Rank order 179
Regression 187-193
Regression coefficient 188
Regression line 187-190
Relative cumulative frequency 23-24
Relative frequency 19-20, 202
Relative frequency tables 19-20

Samples 52-60, 62, 68-69, 100-101
    (see also Cluster sampling;
    Random sampling;

Samples (cont'd)
    Stratified sampling;
    Systematic sampling)
Sampling distribution
    of χ^2 120
    of difference between two means 95
    of the mean 56, 59-60, 62-63
Scatter diagrams 167-168, 174-175, 205-206, 209
Seasonal variation 153-155
Semi-averages, method of 150
Semi-interquartile range 47
Semi-logarithmic graphs 134
Significance levels 86-90
Simple aggregative index 141-143, 146
Skew distribution 49-51
Skewness 49, 205
Spearman's correlation coefficient 175, 178-180, 182-183
SPSS 197-212
Standard deviation 41-46, 54-55, 64, 79-81, 90, 205
Standard error
    about a line 190-192
    of the mean 56-58, 60, 65
    of the probability of success 71-73
Standard normal distribution 90
Statistics 52, 54, 60, 62-66, 87, 203, 205
Stratified sampling 55-56
Student's distribution 97
Suppression of zero 132
Surface graphs 135-136
Systematic sampling 55

t-Distribution 97, 230

t-Tests 96-100, 177-178, 180
Tests
   (see Chi-squared tests;
   One-tailed tests; Two-
   tailed tests; t-tests;
   Z-tests)
Time series 149-158
Trend 149-151
Two-tailed tests 88-90

Unbiased estimates 59
Uniform distribution 73-74
Upper quartile 46-47

Value labels 198-199
Variable 13, 42, 68-71
Variable labels 198-199
Variance 41, 100-101, 159-163

Weighted aggregative index
   143-145

Yates' correction 126

Z tests 92-96
Z values 90-91
Zero suppression 132